The Sounding Tree

Voices Along the Razor Wire

Lee Dickenson

Lost Coast Press

Fort Bragg, California

The Sounding Tree: Voices Along the Razor Wire
Copyright © 1998 by Lee Dickenson

Cataloging-in-publication Data

Dickenson, Lee, 1947–
    The sounding tree : voices along the razor wire / Lee Dickenson
        p.   cm.
    ISBN 1-882897-24-2
    1. Prisoners–United States–Social conditions. 2. Prison adminis-
tration–United States. 3. Correctional personnel–United States.
I. Title.
HV9469.D52 1998
365'.6–dc21
                                    98-18684
                                        CIP

Lost Coast Press
155 Cypress Street
Fort Bragg, CA 95437

1-800-773-7782
Book production by Cypress House
www.cypresshouse.com

To Susan Stine — Confidant and Friend

The wall is gone now. Oh, there are sections still standing here and there but most of it lies crumbling at my feet. In its place stands a quaint rustic fence that seems to say, "Come... come... Lean on me." Through you I have found strength and understanding. Someday, perhaps, I shall find the forgiveness I seek. But for now I think I shall just lean on the fence awhile and enjoy the warmth of the sunrise.

Introduction

E verything in this book is true. I've written these stories as I perceived them at the time and as I remembered them. Others who were present may have seen things differently. Originally, I meant to get these things out of my system. I felt that, maybe, if I wrote everything down and read it all from time to time, I would come to understand some of the decisions that were made by me or my superiors. I think it's working, but I'm not really sure yet.

People have misconceptions of what corrections is really like. Thanks to the movie industry, people think we walk around beating inmates with clubs and guns. When I tell them that there are dormitories, not cell-blocks, they look at me like I'm crazy. When I say that we don't carry weapons other than our radios and that we rely on our skill as communicators, they know I'm crazy.

Originally, I thought that if someone asked me about my job I would just hand this book to them and tell them to come back after they'd read it. Then we would talk about what I do. I never thought that I would publish it.

Readers whose impression of corrections comes from Hollywood will probably think I'm lying. Readers in the corrections field will probably recognize themselves and others in these pages. Readers who are unfamiliar with corrections but willing to suspend their disbelief will find these stories enlightening.

Once you enter a facility you enter a very strange world, a world filled with the dregs of society. We deal in negativity here. Every day is filled with denial. We are so conditioned to watching and waiting for someone to lie to us or to try to cheat us that when another staff member needs something, we automatically say, "No." We suspect everyone of being dishonest. And then, at the end of a shift, with the flip of a switch, the opening of a gate or the sound of a bell, we are expected to act like normal, decent people.

We have our own language. That's why there's a glossary in the back of this book. We also have our own rules and our own code of conduct. All I ask is that after you read this, please try to understand. You see, most of us hold ourselves accountable, more accountable than you can possibly imagine.

Iron Mike

The Department of Corrections collects strange people, and I don't just mean the inmates. As in the armed forces, recruits come from all walks of life, from different cultures, beliefs, races, and sexes (no, that's not a typo; you'd be surprised at some of the sexually-disoriented people who work here. Those stories could fill a book all by themselves.)

Mike Dillon is one of the strangest ones. Mike is a very sick man. His sexual fantasy is... No, I think I'd better leave that one alone. I talked with an inmate who once provided Mike with a girl to fulfill his fantasy, and... no, I can't go there either.

Mike got his nickname from the motorcycle gang he supposedly belonged to. If you were to ask him, he would tell you he was a member of one of Connecticut's roughest bike gangs. I never spoke with anyone who saw him riding with a gang, but that's not to say he didn't belong to one.

Mike had a rather nice bike. (I guess it was a nice one; it looked nice anyway. I don't know much about motorcycles, so I can't say for sure.) It was a big Harley. Mike would give up riding before he would ever be caught on a rice rocket. To hear Mike tell it he wouldn't even acknowledge one, or the rider of one, when he passed him on the road. Every now and then Mike felt he had to prove something to the rest of

1

us. On those days Mike would ride his bike to work and park in the warden's parking spot in sort of a show of defiance toward the administration. After a while, I figured out that Mike only did this on days he knew the warden wouldn't be in.

You could always tell Mike's bike because of the license plate. It read "excon." Kind of implying that Mike had served time somewhere. I guess he had in a way, because we sometimes refer to a twenty-year career as doing a twenty-year bid with weekend furloughs. But that too is part of the image. One day when I was working control, Mike came in to get his paycheck. There for the whole world to see, sticking out of his belt, right over his Harley Davidson belt buckle was a pistol. I don't know if he was trying to impress me or someone else, but I do know that after twenty years in the service what I know about guns is that they get people killed. We are not allowed to bring guns into the jail so I told Mike he would have to leave it outside. I guess he was trying to show his disdain for the rules because he just shrugged and handed it to me. Without a second thought I popped out the clip and then jacked the slide to clear the chamber. Picking up the ejected round I placed everything in the drawer and went back to work. Mike never said a thing.

If I had to pick one word to describe Iron Mike it would have to be "pervert." He sure did look like one. Not tall, Mike stood about five feet seven inches and was kind of overweight. Going bald in the front, he wore his hair shoulder length in back. He looked almost fifty but was only thirty-nine or forty. He was rode hard and put away wet.

What convinced me that Mike wasn't all there mentally was that he always tried to get the female staff to sit naked on the copy machine so he could take pictures of their bottoms. The ones who did had a special place with Mike — in his wallet to be shown around whenever he wanted

2

to impress someone. The game was to try to guess who she was.

On the third shift at Gates at that time was quite a crew. There was Iron Mike, Dave Carter, Big Bob Connors, Lou Reynolds and me. Not many, but then we only had about ninety-five inmates then. The lieutenant always stayed in his office with the door closed. We figured he was sleeping but really weren't sure so we just did our jobs and left him alone.

Now, Big Bob stood over six feet tall and weighed almost four hundred pounds. He was so big that when he had control for a post he would swap with someone because he couldn't fit in the chair in the control center because it had arms. Big Bob had been a corrections officer up in Alaska and when the mood took him he would waste the night spinning tales of how real jails were run.

Dave Carter on the other hand was a fitness nut. In his mid-thirties, he was always lifting weights, talking about bodybuilding, or taking steroids. For a while Dave was juicing it bad. Then his heart caught up to him and he quit the juice. He still lifts, but he's lost a lot of weight. At least he's still alive.

Lou Reynolds was another strange one. He had a toupee that looked like a half drowned, longhaired cat sitting curled up on his head. Why he wore it no one ever knew, other than that he was bald. Lou was about sixty, and this was his second or third career. Before he came to corrections he owned a women's clothing store at a local mall. When his wife left him she took the store with her.

Lou fancied himself a cribbage player. He and Big Bob would spend hours each night playing cribbage on the second floor. Lou was convinced that he was the best cribbage player that ever came out of the Marine Corps. We would argue about that, but he was so set in his ways you couldn't tell him anything. Not that anyone really tried. I played Lou a

3

couple of times and beat him bad. He tried to accuse me of cheating, but Big Bob was right there and told Lou that I hadn't. It wasn't that I was good. I'm not. I just got lucky. After about two weeks of losing to me, Lou didn't want to play anymore.

To get back to Iron Mike, he had a habit of looking in other people's lunches to see if there was anything he liked. When he found something good, it was good as gone. When I first got to Gates, I'd heard that this was going on, but I really didn't believe that a staff member would do something like that until the day he commented on what I had for lunch that night. Since this was before I'd been relieved for lunch, I didn't even know what my wife had fixed. The only way Mike could know would have been to look.

During lunch breaks, he would sit and watch everyone eat. When they were finished he would ask if he could have the leftovers. If you were foolish enough to say "yes," he would take this to mean that you didn't mind his going in your lunch bag after you were finished whenever he liked. I was on a diet, so I mostly ate salads. Mike didn't like health food, so I was safe. But Big Bob and Dave were constantly complaining that they were missing sandwiches. These comments were always made in front of Mike, and it was fun to watch his reaction and listen to him utter threats towards everyone about what he would do if he ever found them in his lunch.

After about six months, things really seemed to get out of hand, and Big Bob and Dave decided to do something. One night when we were all on, Big Bob brought an extra lunch which he slipped in the refrigerator when no one was around.

I was already at lunch when Big Bob came in with Dave. Mike had eaten early that night, but no one had seen him since. Bob opened the refrigerator and started laughing. Dave had a look of amazement on his face. "No, he didn't, did he?"

Bob just nodded. After Bob set his lunch on the table he took a second bag from the refrigerator, looked inside and started laughing even harder. Dave laughed, too. There we were, the three of us, Big Bob and Dave laughing hysterically and me sitting with a dumb look on my face. Lou came in, saw the two of them near tears and said, "You didn't, did you?" Bob and Dave both nodded.

After several minutes, Big Bob got up and put the second lunch back in the refrigerator. With a twinkle in his eye, but without a word, he tried to eat his lunch. Every now and then he would look at one of us and bust out laughing all over again. Under the circumstances, not knowing what was going on, I just sat there with a stupid look on my face. Eventually, Iron Mike drifted in and the whole room exploded with laughter. I didn't know what was so funny, but by then I couldn't help laughing, too. Mike pulled up a chair and asked what was so funny. By this time, trying to stop the laughter was like trying to stop Niagara Falls. It just wasn't going to happen. After lunch, we went back to our posts, all of us, that is, except Iron Mike. He chose to remain behind.

A short time later, Mike came up to the second floor to watch the cribbage game. He didn't say anything; he was just drinking a large glass of water. Big Bob, Dave and Lou started chuckling again but they didn't say anything. While we were playing, Dave quietly slipped away. In a flash he was back. The minute he saw Mike, he laughed so hard he had to lean on the wall to keep from falling down. Big Bob and Lou both lost control. Not being in on the joke, I sat there as confused as Mike.

Dave looked at Big Bob and nodded. "The sandwiches are gone, " he said. When Dave left the floor, it seems he had gone back to the break room and checked Big Bob's second lunch bag. Instead of getting angry, Big Bob was almost on the floor in hysterics. Lou had to leave the area, laughing so hard he was crying. After much work, Big Bob managed to tell Mike and me he was tired of someone going through his lunch so he had made "set up" sandwiches from cat food and cayenne pepper! Mike didn't say a word. He kind of smiled, but you could tell he didn't get it.

I couldn't believe it. Cat food with pepper! I couldn't help myself; I started laughing and that set everyone off all over again. Mike mumbled something about us being stupid and left. I was flabbergasted! We didn't see Mike for the rest of the shift.

When the day shift came in, we made sure they all knew. Iron Mike finally got mad with everyone laughing at him, so we had to cool it. The lunches were safe for a couple of weeks, but eventually Mike reverted to his old ways.

Many weeks later the story came up again. This time it was at the Slime Tavern. We'd all been drinking, so tongues were a bit loose. Mike continued to deny he ate the lunch but I thought I heard him say it didn't look like cat food.

More Guts Than Brains

At one time or another, each and every one of us in this department like to think we were personally responsible for doing something great, like saving someone's life. I know I do. Somehow, I don't think that will ever happen for me, but I still try. I have tried to do some great things or things I thought were great, but in all honest most of them were just plain stupid.

On any given day, a corrections officer may face physical confrontation with one or more inmates. We are taught to make every effort to avoid this possibility. After all, people have a tendency to get hurt in fights and the department spends a great deal of money each year trying to teach us how to avoid getting hurt. From my observations, and judging by the number of workman's compensation cases in this department, most of the money seems to be wasted.

There are "comp bandits," officers who fake an injury so they can get compensation leave. Most of these cases involve bogus claims. For instance, one guy claimed to have hurt his back lifting a stack of twelve plastic food trays. Six months after he went out on comp he was on television winning a state weight-lifting title. In another case, a female staff member got workman's comp for tripping over a radiator. The problem was that the radiator was on the ceiling in the area where the "injury" occurred. I have never been out on comp, but that is not to say I haven't had the chance. I never could see the reason for faking an injury just because I felt lazy.

When a fight breaks out, we're taught to make an "all available officers" call on the radio. The call is supposed to summon every officer who is not involved in something which can't be dropped right then and there. Most importantly we are told not to try to stop the fight until more staff arrives. There is always the possibility that maybe it's not a real fight; it could just be a set-up to get you or your keys.

J. B. Gates Correctional Facility is a level II facility, which means that most of the inmates are on their way out the door. They've either served their minimum time or they maxed out, meaning that they completed their entire sentence. Normally, a level II facility is a sweet place to work. The inmates try to stay out of trouble and not draw attention to themselves. But every now and then, life gets interesting.

The only bad thing about a level II facility is that when someone is about to be discharged he has to settle his accounts with the other inmates. Despite what the departmental directives say about bartering, it is a way of life on the inside and inmates will borrow almost anything from one another. The deal is that it's two for one. If an inmate borrows a candy bar, he has to pay back two. If he can't pay back on commissary day, then he is charged with the one he borrowed and two for interest. He now owes three and will have to pay back six next week.

The Gates facility once consisted of a brick two-story building with thirty or so inmates and one officer on the first floor, and sixty-five inmates and a second officer on the second floor. At that time I was assigned to the second floor. I had a full house that day, although I don't remember the count on the second floor ever being below sixty. The offi-

8

cer's station was a desk in the middle of the hall. There was no place to lock up the logbook, my coffee cup, or anything else. And no place to seek refuge if the shit hit the fan. The hallway was L-shaped with about twelve rooms on either side of the officer's desk and a small corridor at one end with another eight rooms.

I have no idea what started the fight, but it was obvious that the fight was for real. I can't remember the poor fool who was on the bottom, but I know who was trying to protect him.

I was sitting at my station when I heard a commotion at the far end of the long hall. I approached to see several inmates standing over another inmate who was lying on the floor. I grabbed my radio and shouted, "All available officers, second floor!" Then, with complete disregard for all I had been taught, I charged down the hall to the rescue. As I neared the fight, I saw one man down and six others kicking and hitting him with what looked like two locks-in-socks, padlocks wrapped in socks and swung like blackjacks. Someone taking a head shot from one of these could end up dead. All I could think of at the time was to cover the downed man's head.

With more guts than brains, I forced myself into the fight and used my body to cover his head. That was really dumb! I had no idea how much a lock in a sock hurts. I took at least three shots in the back plus a couple of kicks. So without any help at all, I was very successful in getting my ass kicked for no intelligent reason whatsoever.

Chuck Daniels sticks in my mind the clearest of all. Chuck was new to Gates from New Haven Correctional. I really didn't know him that well, but word had gotten around that he never missed a fight. What drew my attention — actually it drew everyone's attention — was a hellacious scream. I looked up and managed to catch a glimpse of some maniac running towards us screaming and waving his arms. Without

9

breaking his stride, Chuck leaped into the pile and started throwing people around, trying to get to me.

I wanted to help, but it hurt too much to move. As more staff arrived, the attackers took off. None of us were ready for the downed man's roommate. Culp was a black man over six feet tall and weighing in excess of three hundred pounds and he was lumbering down the hall to his friend's rescue unaware that we had already rescued him. All he saw was his friend down with a bunch of officers standing over him and one officer lying on top of him.

Culp hit us like a bowling ball hits pins. Staff went everywhere. Like a mighty bull shaking off a terrier, he brushed us away. More staff arrived, and everyone piled on Culp. But he wouldn't go down. I managed to get up and I tried to grab hold of his arm when Culp swung his elbow back and caught the side of my face. All of a sudden my vision went to shit and my knees to rubber.

Somehow, by sheer weight and numbers, and without any help from me, Culp was pinned against the wall. Lt. Rogers, the shift supervisor, was yelling for someone to get the handcuffs on Culp. I was trying to get up, but I didn't have it together yet. I did get my cuffs out. Someone held Culp's arms behind his back and — guess what? — the cuffs didn't fit! His wrists were too big. I was fumbling with my cuffs when someone tripped Culp and we all went down.

At about this point, Lt. Rogers was able to convince Culp we were just trying to help his roommate. He stopped fighting, and we managed to get some restraints on him. My mouth felt funny and tasted worse. I felt it and my hand came away bloody. It was about that time I realized I was missing a couple of teeth. I have no idea where they went. I don't remember spitting them out, so I guess I swallowed them.

The staff got the other inmates back to their rooms and the unit was locked down while I explained to Lt. Rogers

10

what had happened. He sent a relief for me and told me to get started on the paperwork. While everybody else got to relive the fight, I had to write an Incident Report and a Use of Force for every inmate I had put my hands on. The other staff involved only had to write a Supplemental Report saying what they did and a Use of Force. I was able to identify most of the assailants by name, so I also had to write the tickets. A ticket is a Discipline Report for breaking a rule. In this case, it was for assault. When I came to Culp's ticket, I wasn't sure what to write. In my opinion, he was only trying to help. I decided to talk to him.

I found him in his room with his roommate. He was sitting on his bed looking sad, like a kid who'd lost his puppy. All he could say was how sorry he was. He kept saying that if he had known it was me behind him, he would never have hit me. Over and over he said, "If I knew it was you, Mr. Dickenson, I wouldn't have done it." I believed him.

I told Lt. Rogers that Culp had been just trying to help his friend, and I really didn't want to see him get into trouble. I didn't write Culp a ticket, and he made his release date right on time.

Chuck Daniels went on to become a lieutenant at the state's DWI unit. We became close friends and keep in touch from time to time. I went to the dentist and now have a partial bridge paid for by the Department of Corrections. I didn't learn anything from this episode. I still charge into fights.

Hector Rodriguez

Not every day is filled with fights or confrontations. In fact, for every fight, a good officer has a week to ten days of normal day to day operations, sometimes longer. Cowboys in the department are officers with less than five years in the department who go looking for fights. They create most of the fights they get into.

As a supervisor, I have learned that people have a tendency to get hurt in fights. It doesn't matter whether it's the officers or the inmates, someone always manages to get hurt. The young cowboys (rookies, John Waynes, or turks) like to sit around in the bar after work and laugh about how they put someone down or hurt an inmate. The sad thing is, what goes around usually comes around. Word spreads from jail to jail about who is fair or who needs an ass whipping. Eventually something will happen and an inmate will have an opportunity to return the hurt. Life's a bitch isn't it?

The department tries to teach us that through communication we can successfully avoid physical confrontation. The idea is that we should use our I.P.C. skills. These inter-personal communication skills have been proven to work both in police work as well as corrections. I.P.C: the art of listening and speaking intelligently. And believe me, it is an art!

Some officers believe that success is achieved through

fear and intimidation. They work out every day and build their bodies into an Incredible Hulk. Their logic has it that if you are a muscle monster, the inmates will be afraid of you. I have yet to meet a man whose biceps stopped a battery from hitting him in the back of the head. Inmates do that. They'll use a bar of soap, a lock in a sock, a battery, or maybe a rock. When your back is turned, or the lights are out, muscles don't do a hell of a lot of good. It is common knowledge that if the inmates want you they will get you.

I have met officers — young, full of vinegar, juiced up on steroids, more muscles than brains — who are afraid to walk a block by themselves and would never dream of doing it when the lights are out. I have also met those who could go anywhere — lights on, lights off, alone or with someone else. They get respect, but more important, they give it. They give it to everyone, no matter what their crime was or how long they've been in jail. These are the officers who usually have fifteen to twenty years in the department. Either that, or they're in their forties or fifties, retired military, and have learned how to survive. I think that maturity has been the key not to my success but to my survival. If I get out of this job alive, I'll consider myself a success.

I only had about three years in when I met Hector Rodriguez at Gates Correctional. By this time, Gates had opened a second building consisting of two large dormitories and a common room which doubled as the dining room. Each dorm held one hundred inmates. The only nice thing about the dorms was that each one had what was called a bubble — a medium sized room with reinforced Plexiglas windows — used as the officers' station. It allowed the officer a place where he could close the door and have a few minutes of peace and quiet and still see what was going on.

I had only three years service to my credit, but with twenty in the Navy, I figured I had the ability to look at things intel-

13

ligently. Hector was a good worker, and I used him as a tierman whenever I needed something cleaned up in a hurry. A tierman is an inmate worker. The name comes from the old jails, which had rows of cells three or four levels, or tiers, high. An inmate cleaner was called a tierman. Hector never caused trouble or refused to do anything. He had been in the system most of his adult life and knew how to play the game. So I had to admit that I was surprised when he came back from lunch all pissed off.

I wanted to know what the problem was but it wouldn't be right to call him to the officer's bubble and question him in front of everyone so I sought him out. By going to him I was saying that our talk would be as equals. What an officer does and how he does it can sometimes say more than the words he uses. I had to convey to Hector that my concern was genuine.

When an inmate talks to staff it can be misinterpreted as snitching someone out, so it is important for them to maintain some distance and to speak loud enough to be overheard. I was careful to choose the meeting place, settling on his cubicle.

Now we each have what we call personal space. We may not ordinarily be aware of it but when someone enters our space unbidden we become conscious of it. For an inmate, personal space usually includes the bunk area, cubicle or cell. Keeping this in mind, I didn't really enter Hector's cubicle but stood by the entrance so that my intentions would not be misunderstood.

I asked Hector what the problem was, and he told me that it really didn't concern me. I was just an officer and couldn't help him anyway. I asked him to try me; maybe there was something he was overlooking. Hector blurted out that all he wanted was to get transferred.

Hector was from Bridgeport and had been transferred to Gates by mistake. Gates is out in the middle of nowhere.

14

Public transportation here is science fiction. Being city people, Hector's family didn't own a car and without a car they couldn't visit him. To an inmate who depends on family, this can be catastrophic. I told Hector to talk to his counselor and that a transfer was not unreasonable. It was with great bitterness that he then told me about being jerked around.

As I said, Hector was a good worker. He knew that to get something you had to give something in return. In his case it was his work. He had written to Mr. Carlson, his counselor, about a transfer and was told by Carlson that he would be put in for one. Several weeks went by and nothing happened. Hector went back to Carlson who told him that he had forgotten but would do it that day. What Carlson didn't tell anyone was that he was going on vacation, and in his excitement he'd forgotten to take care of Hector. When he got back from vacation, Hector confronted him and Carlson tried to bullshit him with some song and dance. Hector let him slide because Carlson said he would do the paperwork that afternoon and Hector was still willing to try the system. Weeks passed, and again nothing.

Hector told me that he went to the captain and asked for a transfer and was told that it was no problem. The captain told Hector that he would make a phone call and the problem would be solved. Now, at that time, a captain had the power to get anyone transferred anywhere. But nothing had happened. I couldn't understand what the problem was. He was after all a good worker and not a troublemaker! That was it! No wonder he couldn't get transferred. He wasn't a problem inmate.

I had a brainstorm. Motioning Hector closer, I quietly shared my idea with him. He seemed a bit dubious but agreed to think about it. What he really wanted was a chance to talk it over with his friends. After all, I was a c/o and not to be trusted. But what did he have to lose; he was already in jail. The worst that could happen was that my idea wouldn't work and they would keep him here. I returned to the officer's bubble, poured a cup of coffee and waited.

About fifteen minutes later I heard a loud noise down on the block so I hurried out to investigate. As I approached the end of the tier, I saw Hector standing in the middle of the hall, yelling at the top of his lungs. I started to approach him slowly when he yelled, "Get the fuck away from me!" I tried to speak, but he kept yelling at me, telling me to get fucked and that he was going to fuck up the first person who came near him. I tried to reason with him, but he picked up a trashcan and threw it across the tier (careful not to hit anyone). That's when I called for "all available officers."

When more staff arrived with Lt. Infanti, Hector was still yelling at everyone to stay away from him. Lt. Infanti started to move towards Hector when to everyone's surprise Hector just stopped and put his hands up and said "It's over, I don't want any trouble." One of the officers applied the handcuffs and started walking Hector out to segregation.

Lt. Infanti asked me what happened and I told him I didn't know. "Everything was quiet then all of a sudden all hell broke loose." Infanti told me to get Hector's things packed up and sent down to his office. Hector was being transferred. Of course, being a good officer, I did as I was told.

That was the last time I saw Hector. About three years later, after I had made lieutenant at Hartford Correctional, I was stopped in the hallway by an inmate. He asked if I remembered him but I didn't. He said that, thanks to me, he had gotten transferred to Bridgeport. Everything had gone like we planned, no one got hurt, and he'd gotten a ticket for causing a disruption and had been transferred.

I remembered him. "Hector Rodriguez," I said. We laughed for a little while, then he went on his way. He told me that if I ever needed anything, all I had to do was ask.

Sometimes things do work out all right.

Numbers Not Names

I screwed up. Had I done what I was taught, it would never have escalated to a physical confrontation. Luckily, no one got seriously hurt. An ego or two got bruised along with some ribs, but everybody went home at the end of the day, thank the Lord.

Correction officers are taught right from the beginning that you locate an inmate by his number, not his name. I have been in facilities where there are two, sometimes three, inmates with the same name. There may be a couple named Jose Cruz, Manuel Rodriguez, Charles Moore, Anthony Washington, or Michael Smith. When I was at Niantic, we had a Mary Williams, a Mary Butler Williams and a Mary Anne Williams. It can get a little confusing at times, particularly visiting times.

Someone comes to the visiting center window and asks for Mary Williams. Now this wouldn't be too bad except that she doesn't speak very good English and I am not bi-lingual. I ask for an inmate number. She hands me her social security card. I try to explain that what I want is the inmate's number. She looks at me like I'm crazy.

"What unit is she housed in?"

"Niantic."

"I know that. I'm hoping for a housing unit or something."

"Unik? No unik, Niantic."

When all else fails I have to go through each Williams' visiting card to try to find out which list this visitor is on. Do this a half dozen times a day and it gets a little annoying.

Anyway, I was working "A" dorm at Gates Correctional Facility (I don't know why I mention that; I always work "A" dorm. I hope that someday they rename it after me. That would be poetic justice; the one place I hate bearing my name), when I received a call from one of the counselors informing me that C. Moore was being discharged. Now I knew Charley Moore. A nice quiet kid who never created problems for me, always easy going, so I was kind of happy to see him getting out. I went down to his cube and told him, "Pack your stuff, you're out of here." When it was obvious that he didn't understand I told him that the counselor had called and told me to get him ready to travel. He was going home.

Now this made Charley pretty happy. He bagged his property up, gave his commissary away, said all his goodbyes and happily strolled down to the a/p room. This is where inmates are admitted and processed into the facility and where, when their discharge date has arrived, the process is reversed. About an hour later I get a call from a/p informing me that Moore was on his way back to the dorm. I was a little surprised, but I figured that maybe his ride hadn't arrived yet. When Charley came in I asked him what had happened? He told me it wasn't him; it was Clarence Moore who was leaving. I apologized for the mistake and then called the counselor. I told him to be a little more specific when he called for someone next time. When he started arguing with me, I just hung the phone up and went to find Clarence Moore.

Clarence was already packed and ready to travel. I sent him to a/p and went to find Charley again to see if he was all right. Needless to say he was a little upset. It seems that not

18

everyone wanted to give his commissary back. Most of them did but not everyone. Most of Charley's friends were pretty mad and since I was part of the problem I felt that I had better get out of sight while folks calmed down. I returned to the bubble to lay low for awhile.

The bubble is exactly what the word implies. It is a small enclosure with glass all around. The telephone, logbook, desk, and radio are all kept there. Also there is the coffeepot and a small bathroom. We're not supposed to use the bathroom unless another officer is there to watch the floor. Unfortunately there is seldom anyone around to relieve you. So there I was trying to maintain a low profile when another officer showed up.

James Young was a retired navy man like myself, and I felt we had a few things in common. However attitude towards inmates was not one of them. James was trying to make a name for himself as Lt. Infanti's "yes" man. Whatever Lt. Renaldo Infanti wanted, James saw that he got. Infanti's favorite quirk was antenna wires. The inmates would take a piece of wire and string it between their televisions and the false ceiling for better reception. When Infanti came around, he would hit the roof over those damn wires. Then he would reprimand the officer on duty for not getting them down.

I'd tell the inmates that I really didn't care about the wires but that they had to come down quick whenever the lieutenant came around. Reception at Gates was terrible. Inmates needed the wires to get any reception at all, and they didn't like to give them up or have them taken down. If staff took them down, then they were gone. But James was trying to make points.

Without letting me know beforehand, he started down the tier pulling down wires. The inmates knew he liked to do this and that he especially enjoyed it when the inmate's property fell on the floor. Knowing this, some of them tried to get their wires down before James got to them. Unfortunately, one of the first things he saw was Charley putting up his antenna. Charley tried to get it down before Young got to it, he moved a little too slow so James reached over and yanked the wire down for him. When Charley tried to apologize, James told him he hadn't moved fast enough so he was shit out of luck. James coiled the wire up and started walking away. Several inmates followed him saying that his actions were uncalled for and that under the circumstances he should give the wire back.

When James got to the bubble he had a little smile on his face. "Really cranked them up, didn't I?" he said.

I shook my head in disgust and told him maybe next time he should check with me before doing something like that. I also suggested that maybe he should leave, as things were already tense.

He declined, saying that if they didn't like it, then tough. "Don't put the wires up and I won't have to tear them down." At this point, several inmates came to the bubble and asked for Charley's wire back. James said no. One of the inmates tried to explain to James that Charley wasn't himself right now and that it really wasn't his wire anyway. Charley had given his wire away and another inmate had been nice enough to loan him some more.

"Life is a bitch," James said. "It's contraband and he shouldn't have it anyway."

From somewhere, another inmate came up with a piece of wire and tried to hand it to Charley. James grabbed it out of the inmate's hand. He grabbed it back and all hell broke loose.

Punches came from everywhere. I saw James get hit in the head and then he went down. I was trying to get to him but found myself on the floor with someone on top of me. I don't remember Jan King showing up but she was there. Somehow

20

she had managed to make an "all available officers" call before she was jumped. What happened to Jan I couldn't see.

Somehow we lost the bubble. We figured later that there had to be at least fifteen people in a room designed for four. I was down, James was down, and I didn't know where Jan was. About then, the Cavalry arrived. The inmates dispersed and we just lay there for a minute. Jan was on the floor just outside the bubble. It seemed that several inmates held her down while others fondled her. James was on the floor next to me. He had several bruises on his face and was moving real slow. I had taken several punches to my back and shoulders but was definitely in much better shape than the others.

Infanti and the other cops took control of the unit and we left trying to figure what went wrong. We were able to identify several of our assailants, so transfers were the order of the day. It wasn't until much later that I was able to return to my unit. Infanti said I didn't have to go back, but it was something I had to do. When I got there I told the other officers that this was my post and they could leave. They didn't want to, but I made them go. I had to prove that I wasn't afraid. I wasn't. I was terrified.

I took a deep breath and started on my rounds. I knew that everyone was watching me so I made it a point to speak with several inmates. As I came to Charley's cube he motioned me to come in. I was leery but entered anyway. In a quiet voice Charley asked me if I was all right.

"Yes," I said. "I'm a little sore but other than that I feel fine." As I was leaving, several other inmates approached and wanted to know what was going on. I told them that everything was cool, this was my unit and that everyone could just settle down. It was over and we were back to normal.

As I was starting back to the bubble another inmate approached me and softly said, "You weren't the target. We didn't want to hurt you." He kept on walking.

It wasn't until I was on my way home that I figured out what he meant. When I was down, someone had been sitting on me. They didn't want me to get up. The blows I had received were just enough so that I would be sore and able to say I had been beat on. Who or what had determined that I was not to be hurt I have no idea. I did learn a very valuable lesson though. The inmates do know who is fair and they know who needs to get an ass whipping. They are quite capable of taking care of both.

It should be a lesson to everyone. You can do your job and still be fair. You can be strict as long as you are consistent. What you are today you had better be tomorrow. And just a word of advice, be sure you know who is being called for. Get a number. If you're not sure, call the person back. Look at your inmate card. See if the dates jive. This wouldn't have happened if I had got all the right information before I went looking for an inmate. Charley wouldn't have given his wire away and the other inmates wouldn't have jumped in.

James Young became a captain. He now teaches new staff at several different facilities. One of the classes he teaches is inmate recognition. He uses this incident in his lesson plan. Of course he changed it a little to suit his needs, but I don't mind. At least he tries to teach others how to avoid it.

Androids

I have been called a lot of names in life, some of them not very nice. And there have been times I probably deserved all of them. But Margaret Bitterman was different. Margaret was quite a few bricks shy of a full load. She had been in and out of Norwich State Hospital so many times you would have thought it was a motel. The only reason she was at the Niantic Correctional Facility now was that she had been picked up for vagrancy. Because she wasn't a discipline problem and the medical staff knew her back ground as a nut case she was housed in the mental health unit.

The mental health staff, as usual, had no idea what they were doing or what to do with Margaret, so they did what they do best and decided not to do anything. Instead, they arranged for Margaret to be transferred to Norwich State Hospital. In Margaret's case this was like going home.

I had never met Margaret before but that was to be expected since I don't hang out in mental institutions. I will admit though that there were days when the people I worked with felt I should be a permanent resident at one.

I was lucky that day, or so I thought. The shift supervisor, Lt. Norma Elliot, felt that with Margaret's instability perhaps two experienced staff should do the transporting. Jan Collins and I were assigned to the trip. Jan is everyone's idea of the perfect grandmother, always cheerful, nice things to say about everyone, always optimistic and an absolutely fantastic person. When we drew the trip we just knew that it was going to be a piece of cake.

We collected our restraints, searched our vehicle and proceeded to the mental health unit, better known as Davis II, or D-2, so named because it was on the second floor of Davis Hall. Unlike most of the inmates in D-2, Margaret was not drugged. The nurse on duty said, "She's fine, just a little confused." I don't know if she was talking about Margaret or herself.

Margaret had really taken to D-2. It was nice and quiet up there, laid back and easy going, as if everyone, staff included, was on a double dose of Prozac. That had to be it because it couldn't be the food. I've eaten there and, believe me, the food sucks.

When an inmate is transported to another facility, the department requires restraints. Depending on the inmate and the destination, the transporting staff determines what the inmate will wear. Based on what D-2 staff had to say, Jan and I felt we could get by with handcuffs and leg irons. After much discussion with Margaret and with the help of the staff, we convinced Margaret that she was going for a car ride and that, in order to go, she had to wear the restraints. She finally agreed. Normally, leg irons and belly chains would be the order of the day for a mental health inmate but since she was "not going to be a problem," we stuck with the handcuffs and leg irons.

As we left Niantic, we gave the appearance of a happy family on a day's outing, except for the fact that Margaret was behind the cage. So, Jan and I were shocked when out of the blue Margaret called me an android. Her logic escaped us and we both said so. Margaret said it had to do with the fact that I did what I was told. I tried to explain to her that when a lieutenant tells you to do something, the intelligent thing is to just do it. Unfortunately for me she wasn't having any of it and for the next twenty minutes Jan and I tried very hard to convince her this was going to be a pleasant trip and she would have fun.

When we arrived at Norwich State hospital, Margaret seemed to change a little. She thought she recognized the place but couldn't be sure. I should have realized we were in for it when it took us about ten minutes to coax her out of the car. She was hesitant but eventually co-operative. It was only when we entered the building that all hell broke loose. With no warning at all, she brought both hands up together and struck Jan on the side of her temple with the handcuffs. Jan went down like a dropped rock. I grabbed Margaret and pulled her away from Jan. She resisted, so I took hold of her right wrist and tried to apply a pain compliance hold. This is good as long as you have someone with you to grab the other hand. Since I didn't, Margaret raked her nails across the backs of my hands ripping long deep gashes. At this point I decided that we were going to need some help so I did the only thing I could, I yelled, "Help!"

Margaret and I wrestled around on the floor for what seemed like forever. Jan was still out of it but I was holding my own. When security arrived, all they saw was the blood — my blood. Being the highly trained professionals they were, concerned about AIDS, they decided not to join the fray. Jan regained her senses about then and we managed to pin Margaret on the floor. I told security what I thought of them. A medic arrived with a gurney and with the assistance of those highly trained professionals we placed Margaret on the gurney and strapped her down. A nurse showed up and said Margaret had to be moved to the third floor, so away we went. Ever see about eight people and a gurney try to squeeze into an elevator? It's a bit crowded. And all I heard

25

were Norwich State Hospital staff yelling about the blood and to be careful. In the most diplomatic way I could I said, "Shut the fuck up, the blood is mine, not the inmate's."

After Margaret was sedated and the restraints removed, I asked one of the nurses where I could get my hands looked at. She told me I would have to go to a regular hospital. "They can't treat you because you're not part of our staff." After much argument I was at least allowed to wash my hands and apply some gauze to stop the bleeding. On the way back to Niantic all I could think about was how helpful the hospital staff had been and how I was going to be able to return the favor.

When we got there, I went to the medical unit and got bandaged up. I asked the Med staff what Bitterman's medical history was and was shocked to find that no one knew, so I was told to get a baseline check for AIDS and that I should practice safe sex for the next few years. I was flabbergasted. I couldn't believe that this was all the help I was going to get. What happened to all that crap they told us at the academy about staff support after an incident? As it was, no one would talk to me and none of the Niantic staff wanted me to be involved in any fights because I might contaminate them.

Several months later, Margaret was tested for AIDS and found to be negative. I carry the scars to this day. I remember the fear of being infected, I remember the blood and the fact that no one wanted to be near me. I remember my so-called friends turning their backs on me. But most of all I remember the fear. The fear of taking this home to my family. The fear of not knowing. I was so scared that if it hadn't been for Mike Billings I would have blown my brains out. But that's another story.

And I always thought that androids were inhuman.

Like A Lady

Every successful corrections officer over the years manages to develop little quirks that enable him to perform his job in an exemplary manner. These simple techniques are as unique as a signature. Inmates may not know your name or your face but they know by reputation who you are. More important, they know what you are.

The efficiency of the inmates' communications system rivals that of any major corporation. An incident that occurs at one facility will be common knowledge at another across the state within a matter of hours. Not only can they tell you what happened to whom but also why. Incidents that the department doesn't want the media to find out about are broadcast along the inmates' grapevine at lightning speed. We have a saying in the department that goes something like this, "If you want to know what is really going on in the department just ask an inmate."

I think one of the best styles of communicating I ever saw was used by a very senior officer at the Niantic Women's Correctional Facility named Leroy Johnson. That Leroy Johnson had paid his dues was without question. Leroy had worked at the state prison long before anyone decided to give the inmate rights. He had been a corrections officer back when the inmates had to work. In those days, everyone was locked in cells and if you wanted to get out of your cell you had better have a job.

Leroy had survived the strike of the seventies. He walked when the union walked. And for those who crossed the line, he never had a nice word. An older gentleman, Leroy seldom had time for the new breed of corrections officer. Cowboys he called them. He told me once that they were so hell bent on making a name for themselves they had no idea how to do the job and that if they ever tried some of their stupid antics at a real jail they would get walked out, or get their asses whipped either by staff or the inmates. One thing was certain, Leroy was one of the best.

Anyway, I met him back in 1987 at Niantic. He was just finishing up his career and was enjoying a little peace and quiet at this great laid back hole in the wall. Because the administration thought he was a bit cantankerous, Leroy seldom had a housing unit. He was normally assigned to a driving post. This meant that his normal duties were to transport the inmates to medical, or visits, or the school. He was also the person to respond to any calls for assistance.

People liked it when Leroy was driving. He had this sort of calming effect on the inmates. I guess it was a carryover from his personal life. You see Leroy was also a farmer. Not the kind that grew crops but the kind that raised animals. In Leroy's case it was cows and horses. He would get up at 4:30 a.m. to tend to the stock then report to work at 6:45 for roll call.

He very seldom ate lunch with anyone, preferring to spend his time alone sort of lost in thought. But every now and then he would invite me to meet him and whenever this occurred I knew I was in for a learning experience. Not the kind where you get chewed out for something but the kind where someone shares a bit of wisdom. For me it was always something about wildlife. Twenty years in the navy had left

28

me a little starved for simple knowledge. The things that Leroy took for granted, I was just learning. There I was, forty years old, trying to learn things that this man learned as a child.

Niantic was a fantastic classroom. Imagine if you can almost a thousand acres of land where hunting was strictly prohibited. No one was allowed to bother any of the animals so we had a chance to watch them in their natural environment. Whenever I would see something I wasn't sure about I would mention it to Leroy. A couple days later he would call me and tell me to meet him somewhere on the grounds for lunch. In short almost simple sentences Leroy would expand on the subject I had brought up earlier. Sometimes we would walk back into the woods to find a nest or a burrow. Other times we would just sit in the truck and wait for an animal to come along. One of the most fantastic things I learned was how to approach a skunk and not get sprayed. This man knew everything there was to know about hunting, fishing, and just plain living. But when it came to troublesome inmates I think he was the best.

The Niantic women's facility was a strange place to work. Originally called the state farm for women, it was designed to house abusive wives, prostitutes, thieves, and your occasional vagrant. Today it holds drug dealers, murderers, prostitutes, child abusers and terrorists. I forgot to mention the thieves, vagrants, protestors and drunks.

The really sad thing about the place is that someone forgot to tell the administration that with the change in inmates you also have to change the way you run things. Most of the senior staff just couldn't realize that times were changing and they needed to change too. These were no longer the days of misunderstood girls.

As I said before, one of Leroy's jobs was to respond whenever an inmate started fighting with another or with staff.

The perpetrator was usually moved to the segregation unit for a couple weeks. Very seldom did an inmate go peacefully. What usually happened was extra staff arrived and piled on the inmate, put her in handcuffs and leg irons and dragged or carried her out of the building. Sometimes this also meant dealing with her friends if they felt we were being too rough.

One day Leroy and I both had driving posts when a call for assistance came over the radio. The location was Trumbull South. The building had been named after Faith Trumbull, whoever she was, and was used to house mostly sentenced inmates. The north side was for unsentenced inmates.

By the time I had emptied my vehicle and got to the Trumbulls, the combatants had been separated and some semblance of order restored. The only problem we were facing was that one of the participants decided she wasn't going to segregation without a struggle. We waited for the lieutenant to arrive so that we would have a supervisor on scene when we took the woman down. That was when Leroy arrived. Leroy spent a few minutes with us, then with the lieutenant. After that he motioned the assaultive inmate into the dining hall so they could speak quietly.

Less than two minutes later the inmate walked out and headed right for Leroy's truck. The lieutenant mentioned restraints but Leroy told her that they weren't needed. Leroy drove the inmate to seg and she was processed without incident. Everything returned to normal and we finished the day without further incident.

A couple of days later I caught up with Leroy during lunch and mentioned the incident. I told him I was a bit curious about what he and the inmate had talked about in the dining room. At first he didn't say anything, but just before we went back to work he told me he had told her she had to go to segregation and that was all there was to it. The question was, how was she going? Was she walking out that door like a lady with her pride and self respect intact or was she going to be dragged out like a piece of shit? Either way in a couple of minutes she was going.

Several years later, after I became a supervisor, I decided to try Leroy's technique. I have to tell you honestly that it works. It doesn't matter if the inmate is male or female. If you just give them a chance to maintain a little self respect you can work miracles.

Pearl Porter

You meet all kinds in this job. That's what I was told right from the beginning and it was probably the truest statement I have ever heard. When I took this job I thought it meant men, women, gays, straights, cross dressers, murderers, drug users and you name it, but I wasn't ready for Pearl. Twenty years in the navy had not prepared me for Pearl. Hell, I couldn't even spell hermaphrodite, let alone believe they really existed. Boy was I in for a surprise!

I was working at Niantic as a corrections officer and had transferred there on the advice of a friend of mine. He told me if I wanted to advance in this department I would have to prove I was versatile and could work anywhere under any conditions. Welcome to the state's only female correctional facility.

The staff was mostly female. Men weren't really wanted there because it was believed that the men who worked at Niantic were just there for sex with the inmates or to beat on them for fun. Like I said, there are all kinds in this department. Most of the female staff preferred the company of other women and looked upon us men as competition. I really didn't care who liked whom. I was married and not into an abuse thing.

My big drawback was that I had worked other places and

had some idea of how the system was supposed to work. Inmates were inmates, they were not your friends. You're not supposed to be concerned about hurting their feelings. You're supposed to do your job and nothing more.

The staff at Niantic did not believe they had any bad girls there. In fact some of the staff bragged about knowing these inmates from the street. One supervisor told me that one girl had been coming here for the last twenty years and that "she wasn't a bad girl, just misunderstood." A twenty year professional inmate! Now that's about as stupid as the expression, "I'm just trying to find myself." My reply to such a profound statement is, "Go look in the goddamned mirror."

I saw staff bring in dishes they had made at home for the inmates. Birthday cakes, candy, balloons, all kinds of stupid things. The department says, "You will bring nothing in or take anything out for the inmates. " I guess that didn't apply at Niantic. When I questioned an officer about it I was told that "she (the inmate) has been here forever, she's part of the family. It wouldn't be right to not get her something for her birthday."

In exchange for these little infractions the inmates had pet staff. The inmates would knit sweaters for the staffs' children, afghans, make stuffed animals, draw pictures and so on. One inmate had her boyfriend do repair work on staff cars when it was needed. Another had her husband do remodeling work. Hell of a system.

Anyway back to Pearl. Pearl was about five feet five inches tall and weighed well in excess of two hundred and fifty pounds. A short dumpy black woman whose personal hygiene was non-existent and who was missing most of her front teeth. The way she liked to fight I think she just ran into one fist too many. The fact that she didn't believe in showers was obvious as soon as I met her. Her clothes were ratty and dirty, almost like she had lived in them for a year or two.

Now the rules say that all new admissions will be subject to a search, a shower, de-lousing, and a physical. Fortunately for the staff Pearl wasn't having any of it. Because she wouldn't comply with admission procedures, she was placed up in D-II in an isolation room for the night.

On this particular day I was assigned to a driver post. Being the primary driver was a prestigious post and I was determined not to give anyone anything to complain about. I was making my usual stop at medical when I overheard the nurses saying that there was an inmate up in D-II who was refusing to be processed. Knowing that eventually I was going to have to get involved, I took it upon myself to go up to D-II to inquire what the problem was.

The officer up there told me that the problem inmate was Pearl Porter. The name meant nothing. The officer went on to say that she always refused admissions. I asked how she got away with it and was told that no one really wanted to fight Pearl so they would wait until the right supervisor came in and with the lieutenant's permission admissions would be overlooked. Oh, so we have a prima donna here!

The lieutenant on duty that day was a new guy named Robert Galloway. He came to us out of the New Haven Correctional Center. He wasn't happy at Niantic and really didn't want to get involved with the women. He was a professional photographer by trade and had a business on the side. Dealing with Pearl was a decision for the lieutenant, so I hit the road. Maybe an hour later the call came. All available officers, D-II.

When I got there the post officer told me that Pearl had spread water all over the floor of her room, had pulled the electrical wires out of the wall and threatened to electrocute anyone who entered. An all-available was broadcast, meaning all available officers, including the shift supervisor, were to make their way here. I waited for the lieutenant and when he didn't show I called maintenance and requested an electrician on the double. Other responding staff started to arrive, but they were all rookies. I found out later that none of the experienced staff wanted to have anything to do with Pearl, so they all found things to do when the call went out.

I kept waiting for the lieutenant but he was nowhere to be found. When the electrician arrived I told him we were going to need to power off in the east wing. The electrician told me it wasn't necessary, that as soon as she touched those wires to the water it would trip the breaker. I told him to turn the power off anyway. I didn't feel like testing his theory. I really didn't mind a fight at that time, but doing it with rookies was not the best way to win.

Still no lieutenant. As I was starting to tell the rookies what they could expect, I got a very pleasant surprise. An old friend, Chuck Daniels, stuck his head in and asked if I had a problem. I just laughed and said, "Not any more. Welcome to the party." Following Chuck into the room was another officer whom I didn't know. I looked questioningly at Chuck and he just said that the guy was okay. That was good enough for me. The problem was that Chuck and the new guy were from the Gates Correctional. This wasn't their party and technically they weren't supposed to be there. When I mentioned that to Chuck he just laughed and said he was in the neighborhood and just thought he'd stop by. Deep down inside I was real happy. Chuck and I had rolled around on the floor from time to time and we both had faith in each other.

I went back to addressing the rookies. I told them we were going to rush Pearl. The problem was she was in a double room with bunk beds and we were going to have to work around the furniture. I had the rookies each get two rolls of toilet paper. The idea was that as we rushed her, they were to throw the rolls at her head. I wanted Pearl ducking the toilet paper and not watching me. I would be the first through the

35

door with the shield. What we used then were reinforced Plexiglas shields — either concave or convex. In this case we would use concave. What I wanted to do was pin Pearl against the wall with the shield.

Chuck and the other guy had the restraints. Chuck and one of the rookies would reach around me and restrain Pearl's hands. The other guy and the other rookie would go after her feet. I didn't relish the idea of getting kicked in the groin so I told them to make it fast.

Hey, the lieutenant arrived! Robert looked at me and asked if we were ready. Ready I asked? Didn't he want to know what we planned? No, it wasn't necessary. We had done this before hadn't we? Deep down inside I knew we were in trouble. In front of the lieutenant I went over everyone's job with them again. I was kind of hoping he would suggest another option. When he didn't I asked if we were set. When nobody said anything I shrugged my shoulders and said, "Let's go do it."

The nurse opened the door to the room and in we went. The idea was to hit her with the shield and force her backward. If she was too violent then I was to jerk the shield upward under her chin, snapping her head back and causing her a great deal of pain. I hit that woman going full speed and she never moved! As I was thinking oh shit! everyone else hit me from behind. Sheer weight forced Pearl backward right into the bathroom. Imagine please six people fighting in a bathroom. To top it all off the nurse was in there yelling at us that we were going to hurt her. As for the lieutenant? He was there somewhere making sure we didn't use excessive force.

Chuck was trying to grab her hand or arm, but we had no room to move so he was trying to reach over me. I yelled at Chuck to get her! He said he was trying. Somehow it was decided we would force her down to the floor by weight. The next thing I knew, Chuck was trying to climb over me. He was on my shoulders and I was the one going down. As much as we tried, Pearl wasn't moving! I couldn't believe it! Never had anyone ever fought us so hard. She just wasn't going down. She didn't but I did, shield and all.

Somehow they got Pearl out into the middle of the room and on the floor. The restraints were applied and we just sat there for a moment to catch our breath. I looked to see if anyone was hurt but it didn't appear so. Chuck was just sitting there with a big shit-eating grin on his face. It was only after we dragged Pearl out of the room that I got a chance to look in the bathroom. No wonder she would not go down. She was sitting on the sink.

We walked her down to the west wing where there were strip cells. This was to be Pearl's new home. The challenge now was to get her out of her clothes. We only accomplished it because she was already restrained. I left the room with the other guys and allowed the nurse and female staff to take care of that. When they got to Pearl's underwear all hell broke loose again. We charged in and piled on. It was then that I discovered what this was all about. Pearl was a hermaphrodite. Half-male and half-female, she was mostly female with the exception of a small penis. This was not due to a sex change, she had been born that way. We finally got her clothes off and gave her a paper gown for the time being.

While we were doing our paperwork she finally agreed to a shower and physical. Chuck and his friend went back to Gates and I went back to driving.

Later that day I had the opportunity to look at Pearl's record. She had two children! All I could do the rest of the day was to try and imagine what drunken fool would have sex with that!

Two years later, after I had made lieutenant, I received a call from a/p informing me that Pearl was back. I went down to the a/p area loaded for bear. I just knew this was going to turn into a fight again. When I walked in, Pearl recognized me right away. After exchanging greetings, she asked if I was the shift supervisor. When I told her I was, she quietly informed everyone that there would be no trouble. She would complete the admissions process. As I turned to leave, I looked at her and said, "Thanks Pearl, I'm getting too old to fight you." She smiled and said, "Goodnight, Mr. Dickenson."

Five Cents Deposit

Some people will do anything for money. Robert wasn't a crook or anything like that, he was just obsessed with money and he took a fair amount of good-natured verbal abuse over it. When he figured we all had taken a fair shot at him, he would just remind us what he was doing with his money. About then someone always changed the subject.

Robert had retired from the navy as a lieutenant commander. This entitled him to a rather nice retirement check from the government on the first of every month. Working full time for the Department of Corrections, he was drawing another comfortable check. For Robert that wasn't enough. The kicker was that he worked a day's overtime for every day of regular time. This made his department check even better.

But for Robert it didn't stop there. At Niantic, there was always a problem getting time off, and leave it to Robert to find a way to turn this into a money maker. I guess it started with the holidays. Just like in the navy, someone always wants the holiday off. In the navy you can get a stand-by, for a price of course. The bidding usually started at twenty-five dollars. The more important the day and the less lead time, the higher the price. I have seen Christmas go for as high as two hundred fifty dollars. First night in from a long cruise, an even hundred. New Year's or Thanksgiving went for one fifty to two hundred.

Robert was always available. The rate was usually the pay the day would normally draw. Christmas and New Year's drew double time and a half. Everything else was just time and a half. The sweet thing about it was that the money was tax-free for the guy getting it.

The Department of Corrections allows what it calls mutuals or mutual agreements or swaps. This meant that one person would work for someone and at a later date that person would return the favor. Seemed pretty fair. This didn't affect payroll in any way. As far as they were concerned they were paying the person who was listed to work, not the person who showed up. In a way it was a pretty good system. The only drawback was if the person doing the mutual got hurt in a fight. Since this was an agreement between officers I guess if the state wanted to they could withhold insurance payments or workman's compensation payments. I have never heard of this happening but anything is possible.

Robert was resourceful. If someone needed a day off but didn't want to work in return they would call him. The going rate was one hundred dollars cash. No checks, no waiting for payday, you want the day, you pay the money now. The administration either didn't know what Robert was doing or didn't care. I think they knew but turned a blind eye. Robert was after all, an excellent worker.

Now this is a rough guess, but between his retirement, his department check, his overtime and his side occupation, we estimated Robert was bringing in well over one hundred thousand a year. A comfortable amount by anyone's standards, but for Robert, it didn't stop there.

What does a man who brings home over a hundred thousand a year drive? Robert drove a fifteen year old Datsun. When that was in the shop he drove a Ford Pinto. And if that wasn't running, it was something else just as old. It was almost comical watching him come to work. Crunched insides, broken windows, no bumper, one taillight and bald tires. Why he never got pulled over by the police we never knew. But there was no mistaking Robert when he came through the gate.

He would always park this marvel of the modern mechanized world right where it belonged — in front of the trash dumpster. No, he wasn't hoping they would take the car instead of the trash. Robert collected cans.

Connecticut has a five-cent deposit on soda and beer cans and Robert was not about to let that fortune slip through his fingers. Sometimes arriving as much as an hour early, Robert would make the rounds of the dumpsters. I have seen him actually climb into one for a single can. When he saw me he just smiled and went about his business.

Over the next couple of years, Robert expanded his scavenging to include the offices and housing units. He began to come in earlier and earlier. He would check in with the supervisor, then draw a set of keys that would get him around the grounds. No place was safe; Robert was everywhere. He got them all. For fun, some of the staff took to hiding cans or putting them up real high to see how long it took him to find them. It didn't matter; Robert got them all.

Someone commented that maybe Robert should take some cans and buy a new car. It was common knowledge he never spent over fifty dollars for one. Robert heard the comment, smiled and proceeded to pull up a chair. He looked around the room at all of us with a shit-eating grin on his face and asked if we would care to venture a guess how much he had made so far? I had no idea, so for once I kept my mouth shut.

Robert told us that it had taken him a while to figure out what exactly to do with all this money he was raking in. He

41

said that the logical thing was to deposit it in the bank and watch it grow. But that wasn't good enough for him; he wanted it to work for him. The money had to make money. Robert told us that he had decided to invest it in mutual funds. He said that every six months he took his can money and added to the investment and that over the last fifteen years the five cents per can now totaled just under five thousand dollars!

There was a sudden silence in the room. Robert stood up slowly, smiled, and left.

Escape

We are all human and susceptible to life's temptations and pitfalls. When you spend most of your time with the dregs of society eventually some things rub off on you. We all start life with the great expectations of our parents. We're going to be doctors, lawyers, policemen or firemen. No one thinks his child will grow up to be a prostitute, a drug dealer, a bank robber or a murderer.

Marylyn Benning was very attractive and very single, a tiny young lady with two children. In her mid-twenties, Marylyn was very popular among the staff and well thought of. Although she worked first shift, she used to hang around with some of the guys from the third. There were days that she would call in sick just to go over to the casino with the off-going staff.

I can't say Marylyn was a friend because we only spoke during duty hours. She never shared any personal thoughts except where her children were involved and then it was only about baby sitters or school. My only contact with her was when she worked overtime on third shift. I had been on third shift for about a year when I rotated to days as a shift supervisor. Once that occurred I saw Marylyn three days a week.

Sometime around February or March she had what could probably be described as a nervous breakdown. I don't know all the details but I do know that Lt. Miles Dunn and a couple of staff members were called to her house one night by the police. Marylyn was out of work for about a month. During that month she exhausted all her sick time and a note was passed around asking her fellow officers to donate time to carry her over. Without having to ask twice, enough time was donated to carry her for almost two months.

When she returned to work it was as if she had just been on vacation. Everyone greeted her with open arms and pats on the back. She looked a little tired and seemed a little withdrawn but no one ever mentioned it to her.

As I have mentioned, Niantic is a bit different from other places I have worked in that the familiarity between staff and inmates is extreme. Over the next few months, Marylyn started working more and more overtime on third shift. I just figured she was trying to make a few extra bucks to pay the bills. I never really paid attention to the fact that she always asked for the same housing unit. I was just happy that when she was there I never had any problems in that unit.

Anyway, one Saturday morning when everything was supposed to be quiet, the phone rang. One of the visiting officers was calling to report what she thought might be an escape. It seemed that someone had entered the visiting center and asked to see a Nancy Lopez. Since Nancy was housed in Thompson Hall it was going to take a few minutes for her to get to the visits building. The visitor then told the officer that she was going to wait outside. That had been thirty minutes ago!

The unit officer at Thompson Hall had followed procedure and called visits when Nancy left the unit. That was fifteen minutes ago! It didn't take fifteen minutes to walk to visits. What really set things off was a call from one of the on-grounds drivers reporting that she thought she saw someone run out the maintenance gate. When she got to the gate she saw a small brown car with three people in it speeding out on to the main road. The maintenance gate at Niantic was a joke. It consisted of a simple swing type barrier across the road. What compounded its futility was the fact that there wasn't a fence there, just a gate out in the middle of nowhere.

At this point I called for an inmate freeze and a count. All movement stopped right then and there. A count was conducted and I reported immediately to control. Lt. Lynch proceeded to the visits building. As I was being informed that the count was one short, Lt. Lynch arrived and told me that she believed inmate Nancy Lopez was gone. Well if Lopez was gone then she was gone. I returned to my office to notify the duty officer and the state police. What I wasn't ready for was the call from the visits officer telling me that she thought she saw Marylyn Benning driving the getaway car!

That was just what we needed, an escape with a staff member driving the getaway car. The state police arrived and were provided with pictures of Lopez and Benning. At this time we didn't know the identity of the third person. It turned out after a great deal of investigating that the third girl was Nancy's former lover at the facility.

A statewide search was started. Fifteen miles from the prison the girls stole another car at knife point. A search of Nancy's property revealed several love letters from Marylyn. None however mentioned the escape. The state police along with staff from the department proceeded to Marylyn's apartment. When they finally managed to gain access they found the place bare. No furniture, no clothes, no nothing. Marylyn's mother was contacted and we found out Marylyn had given her children away — one to her mother and one to her sister.

Several months later, an inmate wrote a note to the warden informing her that she had been in touch with Nancy Lopez. The girls had made it to Philadelphia and were surviving by turning tricks. Nine months later they were both in custody and on their way back to Niantic. Because of Marylyn's knowledge of the facility she was placed in segregation on a one on one status, which means that a staff member has to keep Marylyn in sight at all times. Because of her association with so many of the staff, only special officers were assigned to watch her.

Since her sentencing for the escape, Marylyn is now housed at the new maximum security York facility. She will be there for the next twenty years or so.

A Little Nuts Maybe, But Not Crazy

Hartford Correctional was a great place to work as a supervisor. All the people I had the opportunity to work with there have moved onward and upward with the exception of myself. The reason for this is that they played the game the way it is supposed to be played. They knew how to keep their opinions to themselves. Maybe I should have stayed there but then maybe not.

The shift commander was Paul Brown. He had been a lieutenant for a long time. It wasn't that he didn't want to be a captain, it was just that he was happy doing his thing. Gifted with a silver tongue, Paul could talk his way out of just about anything, but once he got on a roll there was no shutting him up. He could go on forever about anything. What made him good was that you never knew if he was telling the truth or putting you on.

Next was Jack Bell. Jack was just plain nuts. A two-year lieutenant, Jack could roll with the best of them. He never missed a fight and afterwards he would have this crazy look in his eyes, a look that said, "Let's let the inmate loose so we can fight him again."

Third was Tom Flowers. Tom made lieutenant a month before I did and his goal was to be the youngest captain in the department. He didn't make it. He had a bad habit of pop-

47

ping a shitload of pills. If his stomach wasn't bothering him it was his foot, and if not his foot, then probably his finger. It was always something. He too was a fighter. His idea of fun was to chain someone down and leave them there for a day or two. The department had rules about this, but Tom worked his way around them by cranking the inmate up just before he was due to be released from the restraints. When Tom and the on-coming supervisor went in to remove the restraints, the inmate would start yelling about what he was going to do to Tom when he got free, so the supervisor would have little choice but to leave the restraints on.

Then there was me. I was new to this facility as well as being a new lieutenant. Paul always told me just to stand back and watch how the pros handled things. I didn't mind because when the shit hit the fan it wasn't me in charge.

The second shift consisted of Warren Spencer, William Chaft and Bob Leisuré (pronounced lay-shur-a, with a French twist. Bob thought it sounded nice that way). An extremely large black man, Bob lifted weights. His strong point was that he tolerated nothing when it came to the job. He was very soft spoken, but you just had the feeling that this man could hurt you very easily if he wanted to. I saw him pick a man up by his neck with one hand. But I never ever heard him raise his voice no matter how mad he got.

His only weakness was women. Bob loved women. It didn't matter what they looked like, or how old they were. If it was female, Bob was interested. I don't recall him speaking badly about any of them either. He would always smile and comment on some talent or attribute they had. The amazing thing was, they all knew about each other but never ever talked about it while they were working. There was a truce in the jail between them, but on the street I understand things were a little different.

Many a night Bob would not go home until almost dawn. If

he planned to stay out he would say as he was leaving that if anyone called for him, tell them he was over in the dorms working on a problem. Whenever that happened, the other lieutenants would tell me to handle the phone. It didn't matter to me. I would ask Bob who it was tonight, Gloria, Linda, or Denise? Never saying who, he'd smile and shrug his shoulders.

There were some nights that he would come back to the jail and catch a couple hour's sleep in the medical unit. We would have to go down and wake him just before the medical staff came in. He'd say, "Thanks," grab a cup of coffee and head for home.

The second shift always met after work. Hartford Correctional would meet at Ho-Jo's and close the bar down. After that they would retire to the parking lot and finish the night out there. Now Gloria Pená worked in the facility commissary. Her day ended at ten p.m. She'd head over to Ho-Jo's and start drinking until the second shift got there at midnight. About 11:30 she would call the office to see if Bob was coming over. Sometimes she would have to talk him into it, but he almost always went. Some nights when he didn't, she would call around 1:00 a.m. and hit on whatever lieutenant answered the phone. By then she was always drunk so no one ever took her seriously.

One night as Bob was leaving, he left the usual message, he was in the dorms. So when the phone rang about 2:00 a.m. I answered and politely told the lady on the other end that Lieutenant Leisuré was taking care of a problem inmate right now and couldn't come to the phone. She thanked me and asked if he could call her when he could. I took her first name and number.

Sometime after 3:00 she called again. This time I told her that he was just here but had gone down to the kitchen to fix himself something to eat. She said OK and hung up. I turned

49

to Paul and told him that Bob was awfully popular that night. Tom, Jack and Paul all exchanged looks but said nothing.

At about 7:00 a.m. the shit hit the fan. The lobby officer called me and said that a Mrs. Leisuré was here along with her children to see her husband! The officer went on to say that he had told her that Lt. Leisuré wasn't here. She had then informed him that she was going to wait in the lobby until someone in authority came out to talk to her. I quickly relayed this to the other lieutenants. For a few minutes no one said anything and finally Paul called the lobby officer and they spoke for a few minutes. While that was going on, the three of us tried to figure out which of us was going out to tell her the truth. They decided that it should be me since I was the one she had talked to earlier. I said, "No way!"

I had been in a similar situation before at Niantic and I wasn't doing it again. I wanted to know why no one had told me that Leisuré was married. They said it never crossed their minds. "You're all full of shit, " I told them. "I don't mind lying for someone as long as I know what's really going on. But you've got to tell me the truth in advance."

It was about then that Paul said, "I know her. I'll go out and have a word with her." I breathed a big sigh of relief. While he was on his way out to speak with her, the lobby officer called again. "She just cussed me out. She is really pissed. And her kids are acting up." I turned to Tom and Jack and said, "You sons of bitches set me up didn't you?" They both laughed and nodded that they had.

We all waited for Paul to return, but he didn't come back. Tom called the lobby officer for an update and was told that she was still here, only now she was yelling at Lt. Brown. Not speaking to anyone directly, Jack asked how we were getting out of there. I mentioned that I had parked out front and was going out the front door. Jack said that he had, too, but that he didn't think going out that way was such a good idea. Not being the brightest guy in the world, I asked why. Tom pointed out that she was out there and that we had been lying to her all night.

There we sat, three men who spend all night ready to fight with any inmate foolish enough to try us, cowering from a woman and three children. Tom said he didn't care what we did, he was going out the back way. Jack agreed. As for me, well I was going to follow them.

We may be a little nuts but we ain't crazy.

Toni

It was January of 1991 and I had been at Niantic as a lieutenant for about four months. The staff and I were still trying to adjust to each other and we weren't having a lot of success. They were set in doing things their way and I had tasted the sweetness of doing things the right way so we just
weren't getting it together.

Niantic consists of eight primary buildings, six of which
house inmates. There are other support buildings such as
maintenance, school, storehouse and the trailer, used for
family or conjugal visits. All this is spread over almost a thousand acres in southeastern Connecticut. Also on this land
was a small private lake which takes up maybe seventy-five
to one hundred acres. The population was well over six hundred as usual. With twenty officers and one lieutenant we did
our best.

The buildings were constructed from the 1930s to the
1980s and no two were alike. Each was set up to hold a different class of inmate. By class I mean custody status. In
Connecticut we have three classes of inmates: minimum,
medium and maximum. Divided between these three classes
are five levels.

Minimum custody inmates make up the bulk of the population, and they are level ones or twos. These inmates hold

jobs that could almost be equal to that of trustees. They are identified by their green ID cards. They have what is called "walking around" privileges. This means that after checking out with staff they are allowed out of the building to walk to their next assignment.

Level threes are medium custody. These inmates must be transported everywhere. If they are allowed to walk it must be with a corrections officer and they must wear restraints. They can have a job but it is one that requires supervision. They are not to be left unattended. They carry yellow ID cards. Also in this group are the unsentenced inmates. They have white ID cards.

Level four inmates are maximum custody. They can only have a job within the unit where they are housed. They must wear restraints wherever they go and must be transported. Their ID cards are pink. Level five inmates are high risk or assaultive. They too are housed in a maximum-security building and can only be transported singly. High-risk inmates are not allowed to have contact with other inmates. Each possesses an orange ID. Again restraints are a must. ID cards are supposed to be clipped on the clothing where they can be easily seen.

The buildings were broken down as follows. The dorms held mainly minimum custody but there was an occasional medium here and there. The Fenwicks were divided in half. The kids were on one side. These are inmates under the age of twenty-one. The law requires that youthful offenders be housed separately. Unfortunately because of this, all custody levels of youthful offenders were housed together. On the other side were the long-term inmates; those doing fifteen years or more but who are not discipline problems. Again all levels are mixed here, except the high-risk inmates.

The Trumbulls hold only medium custody inmates. Again the building is divided in half. There is an occasional maximum inmate mixed in here and there but mostly mediums. Thompson Hall is the security unit. It holds mediums, maximums and high-risk inmates. The building itself is divided into two sections. Each section consists of two floors. The east end of the building is the segregation unit. This houses discipline problem inmates as well as high risk. The west side holds maximum custody inmates. All the exits consist of an inner and an outer door, one of which is to be locked at all times.

The Davis building is the medical unit. On the first floor it houses any inmate requiring twenty-four hour medical attention. The second floor is designated the mental health unit which houses inmates who can't seem to adjust to the idea of incarceration or life in general. Lucretia Shaw building is for the program inmates — those trying to quit smoking, drugs, or alcohol. Only minimum or medium custody inmates are allowed there. All the units can house un-sentenced inmates but the amount of their bond determines which unit.

I said there were twenty officers. These were spread among all the buildings and also included control and rovers. Not a good ratio of staff and inmates by anyone's standards.

To me Toni Rogers was just a name. She was doing a one-year bid on a third degree assault charge. By average standards this was nothing. A year could be done standing on your head. Or so it seemed to me. She came to us in July but didn't get sentenced until September. This made her release date July of 1991. When she was admitted she weighed only eighty-nine pounds and stood five feet four inches tall. She wasn't HIV positive or anything like that; she was just tiny.

Toni ended up in segregation for creating a disturbance. She was upset about not being able to see someone from medical. She raised a little hell and got fifteen days in the segregation unit. This was on December twenty-second.

Somehow she ended up staying longer than her fifteen days but I have no idea why. At that time we were required to maintain something called a segregation sheet on every occupant housed in segregation. The seg sheet was a way of monitoring the inmate on a thirty-minute basis. This meant that the staff had to look in on her at least every half-hour and make a notation on the sheet. We entered whether the inmate ate or not, took a shower, went to medical, came out for recreation, or requested anything in particular. The supervisor was required to make at least one entry per shift when they toured the unit.

Toni was what is called a "house mouse." That is an inmate who very rarely leaves her cell or room. Most of the time is spent in bed pretending to be asleep. Technically it is a form of severe depression. If she were a staff member I would have called employee assistance to give them a heads up and then quietly recommend that she call them and arrange a meeting. But she was an inmate so I guess she did-n't really matter. It is amazing how callous you can become in this job.

When I first met Toni it was on third shift. She was in the staff office talking with the officer on duty. This in itself was unusual because inmates are only allowed out at night to use the bathroom. At that time it was customary that when the supervisor came in the inmate left. This was done so that the officer could brief the supervisor and discuss any changes in someone's status. Upon seeing her for the first time my impression was that she was HIV positive in the advanced stages. Her cheeks were sunken; she walked with a drugged shuffle and had what a veteran would call "the thousand yard stare." Her eyes weren't focused on anything and her mind was a million miles away.

I looked questioningly at the officer and she just shook her head. After she left, the officer told me she was Toni Rogers.

The name meant nothing so I dismissed her. As this was a problem unit, I was mainly concerned with the inmates with whom I might have to fight. The officer told me that Toni seemed to have just given up on life. Still believing she had AIDS, I said nothing. In this job these things happen. I saw Toni several times after that over the next couple of days and each time she looked worse. I asked when she was going to be moved to the medical unit and was informed by the housing unit officer that they didn't want her there because there was nothing wrong with her. It was only then that I started to take a real interest in her.

I made it a point after that to ask about her every day and to look in on her whenever I was in the unit. Whenever I was in medical I would ask the nurses if they had seen her recently. Most said no and I suggested that it might be a good idea if the next time they were over in seg they spend a few minutes with her. Sometimes this was well received but most times I was told that there was nothing wrong with her so why should they bother.

Missy Lawrence was the officer assigned to the seg unit. It was as a result of Missy's concern that I started to worry about Toni. I told the staff that from now on any contact with Toni had better be entered on the segregation sheets and in the unit log. I told them that I also wanted to know whenever she was sent to medical for anything. Missy and I spoke about Toni several times over the next few days while I was trying to find out what was wrong with her. Missy told me that she (Toni) had just given up. "Bull shit! That doesn't happen. That girl weighs maybe eighty pounds and looks like shit. There is something wrong here and I want to know what." I told Missy to talk to her about her family and friends and find out why she was down like that.

I had the nurse pull her file and tell me if there was anything there I should know regarding her physical condition.

According to medical she wasn't sick but I still wasn't buying that and said so. There just had to be something.

Officer Lawrence called me one night and said that Toni was really sick. She told me that she couldn't stop dry heaving and that blood was coming up. I told Missy that I would send a driver and to get Toni over to medical. I then called the medical unit officer and told him that Toni was on her way.

About ten minutes later I received a call on the radio requesting my presence at medical. When I got there I found Toni leaning against the wall bent over a bucket trying to throw up. The officer was just standing there with a confused look on his face. As soon as the nurse saw me she started yelling at me. "I want this girl out of here and out of here now! There's nothing wrong with her and I'm not going to waste my time conducting an examination."

I asked the nurse to please check her out and if nothing were wrong then I would return her to the seg unit. The nurse refused. Not wanting to create a confrontational situation in front of the staff I asked the officer to help Toni to my car. When we got to seg, I told Officer Lawrence to document everything, all the calls to medical, who she spoke with, what was said, everything!

At that time I had a friend who worked at Niantic as a contract doctor. I spoke with her one day about Toni and asked that as a favor to me would she see her. She assured me that sometime that day she would talk with Toni. I left for the day thinking that maybe now something would get done.

I returned to work that night hoping for the best. I was told by the off-going supervisor that we had one inmate at the hospital. The inmate was Toni Rogers. Yes! Finally someone had done something. As I was making my rounds, I stopped at seg and was told that Toni was in intensive care. All I could do was cross my fingers.

Three days later I returned to work after my weekend. I checked the status board in the lieutenant's office and saw that Toni was still at the hospital. I asked about her condition and was told that she was doing OK; she was hanging in there. Two days later when I came to work, the status board showed no one at the hospital and I figured she was back. I asked the off-going supervisor if Toni was in medical or seg and was told that she was dead. I couldn't believe it! There was no way! I just couldn't believe it. I went looking for Missy Lawrence and found her in the staff lounge, but she was visibly shaken so I waited until we were alone before I mentioned Toni. Missy told me that she had been concerned and knew that I would ask that night so she went to the hospital to check on her. Even though I really didn't believe it, I told her that we had done all we could.

The next day I waited for the doctor to come. I had to know what had happened. The doctor told me that Toni had weighed less than eighty pounds when she was admitted to the hospital and that in her opinion Toni had just stopped wanting to live. Somehow it just didn't seem right. There had to be another explanation. The facility started an investigation. In their opinion somebody had screwed up somewhere and they were determined to affix the blame. Thanks to Officer Lawrence it was determined that no one on the third shift could be deemed negligent. Officer Lawrence had done her job correctly, she had documented everything. I took a few minutes at roll call the next day to tell everyone that we had Missy to thank for keeping us out of it. I stood in the middle of that room, looking right at Missy, and told her thank you. That she had done everything possible and that I knew it wasn't much consolation but she had tried and that was all anyone could ask.

It was never determined who had been negligent. Once again, someone's incompetence had been overlooked or covered up. Toni had a discharge date of July 1991. I couldn't believe it, if she maxed out she only had six months left to serve.

Several months later Missy Lawrence transferred to another facility. Niantic had finally gotten her like it did everyone else who tried to care. Like others before her, Niantic had labeled Missy Lawrence as a problem employee and after a great deal of aggravation and harassment she left state service.

As for Toni, although I had spoken to her from time to time, we really had never talked. Towards the end, I looked in on her every day but in reality I guess I never really saw her. Like so many things in life, I just didn't have time for her. I guess this makes me a contributor to her demise along with so many others who never took the time.

Davis II

Niantic's mental health unit was famous for its fifteen-minute cure. It went something like this:

An inmate would break up with her girlfriend. (Niantic encouraged these relationships in the belief that if a girl was sexually and emotionally satisfied she would not be a discipline problem.) When the breakup occurred, the hurt party would usually throw a tantrum and staff would be called along with a supervisor.

The resident staff in the unit would always be sympathetic to the hurt party and tell the supervisor that she had emotional problems and needed to be seen by D-II. The supervisor, placed in a situation where something had to be done, would usually give in. The D-II staff would hold her hand, give her a cigarette and a cup of coffee and listen to the lover's tale. Then they would call the unit and get the other person's side of the story, let the two of them talk on the phone and make up. All this took about fifteen minutes. Then the girl was sent back to her unit and the lover and the mental health staff patted themselves on the back for another job well done.

Niantic employed what it believed to be the best available staff for its mental health unit. In reality, half of the staff were its best customers. They themselves were involved in such screwed up relationships that they spent most of their time helping each other. When an inmate came up with a real problem they would all sit around with her and compare sad stories. They really believed they were doing something to help the patients. In actuality, all they were doing was giving the inmates insight into staff members' personal lives. Down the road, the inmates would talk about the D-II staff and the story would get around the grounds. When this happened, the wounded party would end up breaking down and have to be relieved due to emotional problems. When the supervisor got involved, he or she would end up with a staff member out sick due to stress. You could never convince them that they had created the problem themselves.

As long as an inmate was well behaved, she could stay in D-II. Once she became a disciplinary problem she was immediately transferred to another unit. After all, D-II didn't have problem girls. If you were to ask any of the staff up there, they would tell you that their inmates weren't really bad girls, they were just misunderstood.

Misunderstood. Right. We are talking about women who sexually abuse their three-year-old children with help from their latest boyfriends. Or women who prostitute their ten-year-old daughter so they can buy drugs. Not to mention the nice sweet twenty-year-old baby baker who didn't want her newborn and didn't know what to do, so she put the child in a gas oven until it died and then blamed that action on her father, or mother, or boyfriend. Anyone but herself.

Then there's the woman who set herself on fire and received massive burns all over her body. She wrapped herself in toilet paper and lit it because of a lovers' dispute. Now she has scars everywhere. According to the mental health staff, she is not suicidal or mental; she doesn't need to be in D-II. She is a disciplinary problem!

Most of the decisions not to house an inmate in the mental health unit were made by nurses and treatment staff, not doctors. The treatment staff were just corrections officers who had taken a bunch of psychology classes. As for the doctors, they rarely came to D-II.

One of the nice things about the staff was that they really believed they were helping the inmates. They believed it so much they would brag about their success rate. Every now and then someone from outside the facility would visit D-II and be impressed with the way the girls were so well behaved. No one ever told the visitors that the day before their arrival the inmates were given a mild dose of Thorazine. They would then slowly walk around the halls smiling and doing what they were told. It sure did look good.

I never did endear myself to the staff up there and I admit that I don't have any training in mental health problems; however, as the shift supervisor I am credited with enough intelligence to recognize a problem when I see one. Should I arrive at a housing unit and see an inmate lying on the floor bleeding all over from self inflicted wounds, it's safe for me to say that she needs to be in D-II for a little while.

This really did happen. I called D-II and told them that I was sending an inmate named Paula Brown up, and why. The nurse told me that it wasn't their problem; I should send her to medical and then to segregation.

First I sent Paula to medical to get bandaged up and then I sent her to D-II. As I was leaving the girl's housing unit, I received a call via the radio that I needed to contact D-II right away. The nurses had refused to admit the girl or even see her. I asked why and was told that they thought she was only acting out to get attention. After about ten deep breaths I got into my car and proceeded to D-II.

When I got there, I found the officer in the hall waiting. She pointed towards the TV room and as I entered I saw Paula lying on the couch in fetal position sobbing. I asked the officer where the nurse was and was directed to her office. I found her seated quietly at her desk reading a magazine. After exchanging pleasantries, she told me that in her opinion the inmate was not a D-II candidate.

"Someone sitting in the dark, cutting themselves on the wrists, arms, torso and neck certainly is a mental health problem and I really think that someone needs to look at the girl."

The nurse told me she didn't think so and that if the inmate was going anywhere it was to segregation. I re-stated my desire to have Paula admitted to mental health. Again the nurse declined.

"I really wasn't asking," I explained. "As long as I'm shift supervisor, I'm responsible for the whole farm." This meant that if I wanted someone evaluated for a problem, she's going to be evaluated.

The nurse admitted the inmate and put her on a fifteen-minute suicide watch. She was only doing so, she said, because I had ordered it. "The next day the inmate will be moved out of D-II," she told me. "I remind you," she said, "that this girl is not a mental health problem. She's just acting out for attention."

"We'll cross that bridge when we come to it," I said. As it turned out, the inmate was moved to segregation as soon as my shift was over. I was told later the nurse on duty felt I was just acting out, trying to exert my authoritarian position. After all I didn't have any training in mental problems and didn't know what I was talking about.

Less than a week later when I returned to duty I received a radio call for a medical emergency in the segregation unit. The inmate's name was Paula Brown.

Deniability

Paula Brown was to be my Waterloo. I never knew Paula, although we had words from time to time. I still feel anger when her name is mentioned, though, anger not at Paula but at the people who contributed to the fiasco.

Paula was a drug user. There were times when she sold herself to support her habit. She only weighed about a hundred pounds. Instead of receiving mental health care, she was in segregation. Why, I have no idea, other than the staff up at D-II were lazy. I never really cared why someone was in segregation except when they fought with one of my officers. It was from Paula that I learned the true meaning of deniability.

Segregation at Niantic was a joke. Most times when you mention segregation the first thing that comes to mind is a cell with nothing in it. But at Niantic that is not quite true. No one at Niantic really knows what a segregation unit is. Those of us who have worked elsewhere know, but the powers that be at Niantic? Hardly. Segregation is not supposed to be a nice place. At Niantic it is a vacation of sorts.

The cells aren't really cells at all. They are rooms big enough for a single bed, a small dresser, radiator, and sometimes a private bathroom. When someone is in seg they are not supposed to have any personal comforts. At least that is what the Department of Correction guidelines says. At Niantic, inmates are allowed to have televisions, radios, books, letters, personal clothes, commissary and cosmetics and whatever else they have. The only thing they give up when they go to seg is sharing a room with someone else.

Paula Brown had been previously housed with the general population but I had her moved to Davis-II. How she ended up in segregation with her previous history still puzzles me. As supervisor, I was required to visit segregation at least once a shift. We were supposed to speak with anyone in the unit who wanted to talk. The usual request was for a phone call, a shower, and a chance to come out and have a cigarette, or to try to pass something to someone else in seg. Most of the time though it was to complain about the officer on duty.

Greg Reynolds was the officer on duty in seg for this rotation. He was a mediocre officer who only did the minimum required of him. That was one of the reasons why he was in seg. You really didn't have a lot to do there. Just make rounds every twenty to thirty minutes, look in on the girls and let out the ones who didn't have a bathroom so they could use the common bathroom. Then make an entry on their seg sheet.

Seg sheets are very important. The officer must log his rounds, note what the girl was doing, if she came out, if she did or didn't eat. Also there is a place for comments. Was she talkative, mad, depressed, whatever. There is also a space on the sheet for the shift supervisor to sign when he or she was in the unit. The fact that Greg kept his sheets up to date didn't mean that he made his rounds or anything, just that he kept them up to date.

Disaster struck at about ten a.m. All available officers! Medical emergency in restrictive housing! My first thought was that someone had tried to cut up — slash her wrists. I conducted a mental inventory of who would be responding and was comfortable that we had things well in hand.

Michael Billings was my primary driver. I depended upon him more than on anyone. We got there at about the same time. Mike had his emergency medical bag in hand. As we entered seg I heard Greg yelling "In here, in here, hurry!" We rushed down the hall to the first open door we found.

I entered Room 5 to find Greg with his arms around the inmate's thighs, trying hold her up. She was hanging from the pipes overhead. I climbed up on the toilet, grabbed her around the waist and tried to lift. It is real hard to lift a hundred pounds when you can't get good footing. Mike climbed up on the sink and somehow managed to free her. She had used the belt from her bathrobe, tying one end around her neck and the other around the water pipes in an attempt to hang herself. Somehow, after a great deal of struggling for decent footing, we got her to the floor. It was then I realized that Mike and I were the only ones in the room. Greg seemed to have just disappeared. Mike couldn't free the belt from her neck because it had pulled itself tight, so using a pair of medical scissors from the emergency bag, he finally got the belt free. He looked at me and I could tell he was concerned, he leaned over to try to hear if she was breathing — she wasn't. I looked at Mike and he shook his head. Mike was an EMT, he knew about these things.

I told him that we would have to try to do something. He started to clear an airway while I began chest compressions. As I was counting I looked up to see the two responding nurses just standing there in the hall. I told them to get in there and help but they didn't move. Mike called for the oxygen bottle. I saw other staff there but I can't remember who. "Radio control," I said, "and get an ambulance in here now!"

I saw Mike open the oxygen bag and he started swearing. Nothing was assembled. I kept working on her chest while Mike tried to put the damn thing together. He finally shoved it across the floor at the nurses and told them to get it together. Meanwhile he went back to mouth to mouth. The nurses couldn't get the assembly together either. Mike then called for an airway. I guess that's what it's called. It is something that goes down your throat to allow a free passageway for air. The nurses didn't have one. Actually, they did, but it was for someone the size of the Incredible Hulk and this girl was only five feet tall and a hundred pounds. If Mike tried to force it in he would have done more damage to her throat than the belt had done.

The ambulance finally arrived along with the fire department and more EMTs. They took over from us but I could see by the way they were working that they knew it was too late. As I left the room I asked the nurses what they were doing there. No one had an answer. I found Greg sitting in his office doing nothing. I wasn't sure what to say to him so I went back to the room. Isabel Jenkins arrived from visits and I told her to be ready to go to the hospital with the ambulance.

As the girl was moved to the ambulance I looked at Mike and he again shook his head. It was then that I heard some of the other girls in seg saying, "We called him and he didn't come. We kept yelling to him that something was wrong. He never came." I told them to calm down, that everything would be all right.

"As soon as the ambulance is gone, I'll be back to speak with everyone, " I assured them.

I went back to the office and asked Greg who it was.

"Paula Brown." I asked if he knew why and he just shook his head. Sometimes an inmate will say something to staff before she hurts herself. It's a way of asking for help. Greg said he had no idea. I asked him if he had been making his rounds and if she was ok on the last check. He told me that she was OK just ten minutes before. I asked him for the seg sheets. I wanted check the last entry on Paula's sheet. There was no indication that there was a problem. But as I was going outside to speak with the medics, one of the girls in the room across the hall told me that Greg never came out of his office.

The medics were standing outside the ambulance when I got there and without having to ask I was told that it had been too long, that she was dead before we had even cut her down. The medics figured that she had been hanging for at least thirty minutes. I just shook my head.

Returning to the office I called everyone together. I told Greg to write the incident report, Mike a page two, Isabel a page two, the nurses also. (An incident report is a form designed by the department. It requires all the names of responding staff, the names and numbers of all inmates involved and most important, what happened, where and when. There are spaces for the number of pages, attached reports and dispositions. A page two is a supplemental report that goes with the incident report. Anyone who is listed on the incident report is required to complete a page two. On it they must state when they arrived and exactly what they did up until they were released by the supervisor to return to their normal duties.)

I told Greg to lock the room and let no one in there. I collected his log and the seg sheets and then proceeded to my office to beep the duty officer. (Every facility has a senior officer or administrator who is on duty or on call during non-normal business hours). I then beeped the warden. When fifteen minutes had passed and no one called in I beeped them again. I then decided to beep the major and the deputy warden figuring that someone would call in sometime. Now all I could do was wait. I called the state police and reported the death. They said they would send some people out to do an investigation. Two hours passed and still no call in. It was then that I made what I believe to be the worst decision of my career.

Rather than have the Brown family get a call from the hospital telling them that their daughter was dead and that the hospital needed instructions on what to do with the body I felt that they should hear from the facility first. I got out Paula's file and placed a call to her mother. When I got through to her I tried to explain what had happened and that the warden or someone would be in touch with more details as they became known. The family was having a party and they had been drinking. After being subjected to an excessive amount of verbal abuse I told them that I had to go and would get back to them soon.

The warden finally called. I told her what had happened and that the duty officer had yet to call in. She didn't believe me. I finally convinced her and she said she was on her way in but that it would be awhile. She had company!

After about an hour and a half, Lt. Mitchell Green showed up. It seems the warden had called her and told her to get in and find out what happened. The warden had also called Lt. Sal Christaldi and ordered him to report to the facility. He was the unit manager in charge of the seg unit. When he protested that it was a holiday and that he had company, she told him she didn't care and repeated the order. Sal got there shortly after Lt. Green.

The warden called in sometime in the afternoon and spoke to Green. Her message was for me. Make sure that all the reports read that Paula had died in the ambulance on the way to the hospital, not while on grounds. We had never had a death on grounds and the warden didn't want to start now. When Sal arrived I was surprised to see him and asked him what he was doing there. He said he wasn't sure, only that the warden had ordered him in. We talked for a few minutes about what needed to be done and he went over to the seg unit to spend the next five hours with all the girls. He let them all out of their rooms so that they could console each other, smoke and just plain vent. I, on the other hand, waited in the office until the state police arrived and then brought them over to the room. They took pictures, we took pictures, they measured, we measured. They took statements; we already had them.

The warden didn't arrive until after 4:00 p.m. About 5:00 p.m. somebody showed up with a bunch of grinders for all of us. The warden figured that we had been working straight through since morning and must be hungry so she had bought them for us. After all it was a holiday and I guess she felt we should have a treat. Some ate but most of us weren't really hungry. By now I had a handful of statements from the other inmates all saying that Greg Reynolds hadn't been making his rounds. I didn't put much faith in them at first, as it is common practice for the inmates to try to blame staff for everything.

When I told Sal about the statements he nodded his head in agreement. He told me that he heard the same thing from the girls. When I asked if he believed them he said yes. He said there were too many consistencies. Although I still didn't want to believe, I had a gut felling that what he said was true. I just shook my head in disgust.

It was 6:00 p.m. before all the reports were done and everyone was satisfied. Everyone but me that is. It was a hell of a way to spend Memorial Day weekend.

I saw Sal on the following Tuesday and he was mad! I asked him what the problem was and he told me he was getting a letter. "A letter, for what?" I asked. He indicated that he didn't want to talk there so we went outside. He told me the warden was going to give him a discipline letter for the suicide.

"I don't understand."

"Because it's my unit and the warden's holding me responsible, " he said.

70

"How could she do that?" I asked. "You weren't even there."

He said he didn't understand either but he was getting a letter anyway. "Shit flows downhill, she told me, and she says she's not going to take the blame for this." He tried to argue with her but the warden had to place the blame somewhere and he was going to be the fall guy.

About two weeks later I was told that a debriefing team would be at Niantic to help ease some of the tension between the custody staff and the nurses. Imagine, two weeks after a major incident, a crisis intervention team was finally showing up. Again all I could do was shake my head in disgust. Those in attendance would be Mike Billings, Greg Reynolds, Isabel Jenkins, both nurses, the staff from D-II and me. It was about then that I was starting to understand. Greg swore he made his rounds. Five inmates wrote statements that they never saw him. Greg said he had no indication of what was going to happen. The statements from the inmates said that Paula had said she was going to hang up. Greg denied everything.

The nurses stated that they saw no reason to get involved. Mike and I were doing just fine. As for the oxygen, it wasn't their job to make sure the apparatus worked. And as for the airway? Neither one of them were responsible for packing the emergency bags. How were they to know that there was only one airway in the bag and that it was the wrong size? After all it wasn't their job.

The mental health nurses from D-II didn't know anything. They didn't even know why they were there. After all Paula was a seg problem. Sure she had been in D-II a couple days before for a suicide evaluation but she had been cured the same day. That was why she was in seg. If she had been suicidal they would have kept her in D-II. But she was just acting out. This wasn't a mental health problem, it was a custody problem.

71

As for me, I was really mad. The duty officer hadn't called in when beeped and it wasn't my job to call the family, somebody else was supposed to do that. The fact that no one was around to do it is of little consequence. I was there and I had made the decision.

The family sued the state and the facility. No one in the administration could understand why. They hadn't done anything wrong. This was just an unfortunate accident. The state settled with them for an undisclosed amount. I found out later what the settlement was and believe me, it was a pretty cheap price for negligence.

Greg left state service shortly thereafter. He said he was stressed out. Mike Billings gave up on custody and became a fire safety officer. Lt. Christaldi retired. Isabel Jenkins tried fighting the system for a while but they finally got to her and she transferred out. A priest had to be called in to exorcise the room and even today the inmates say they see Paula's ghost. As for me, I still try. I still fight the system but I haven't won in a long time. I have been told that I will never receive another promotion. I am, after all, the only supervisor to allow a suicide at Niantic.

Bitter? Yes. I am very bitter. I saw almost everyone involved try to place the blame on someone else. At the annual awards ceremony for the department I asked why none of my staff had been recommended for the preservation of life award. The warden told me it was because we failed.

I started getting harassing phone calls from the Brown family. Finally when I had enough I went to see the warden. The warden had a bank in her office. It was called the f-word bank. Every time you swore in her office you had to place a quarter in the bank.

When I entered her office I reached in my pocket and took out a $5.00 bill, put it in the bank and closed the office door.

"I'm still getting phone calls from the Brown family," I said.

72

"And because of what I've said about mental health and medical, I'm no longer receiving any co-operation from that department." But most important was the phone call to the family. I told the warden that I didn't know who was supposed to make that call, "But sure as shit it shouldn't have been me. I only did it because no one else was around. But you can bet your ass I'll find out whose job it was and when I do I'm going to take them out to the parking lot and beat their ass."

"Actually," the warden said, "I'm the one who is supposed to notify the family."

"Then get your ass out to the parking lot," I told her.

She asked me to step out for a few minutes and while I was gone she called the employee assistance people and said she had a supervisor who was having a nervous breakdown. I was sent home for ten days to calm down. That was four years ago, and I haven't calmed down yet.

When I returned from my ten-day leave of absence there was a blank envelope in my mailbox. Inside it was a five dollar bill.

Stress

They say this job is a little stressful. I think "little" is the wrong word. Extremely stressful maybe. The job takes its toll on you in many ways. Most people end up separated or divorced, depressed or suicidal, addicted to either drugs or booze, and always paranoid.

I was paranoid, depressed, and suicidal and ended up seeing a therapist and taking Prozac. I can't tell you why, because I don't know why. But maybe if you understand what happened to me you'll be able to recognize it in someone else and help him or her avoid it. I hope so, because for me it's been a long three years, and it's still going on!

It started about eight years ago at Gates Correctional Facility. I was working the day shift in the old dorms. We were supposed to rotate every now and then but I always ended up in either A dorm or B dorm. Both sucked. One officer to a hundred inmates. Eventually you start to lose your patience. Then it becomes physical. Your stomach refuses to hold anything down, and then your bowels start to act up. Soon you've got diarrhea so bad that your system voids itself before you go to work, when you get there, and all day long. When you feel the urge to go to the bathroom, you had better start on your way or you aren't going to make it. The older officers knew the symptoms and didn't say anything.

But the rookies couldn't let it go. They would always make some remark or other at roll call. Someday it will be their turn.

My daughters were the first to notice. I was so wound up from work when I got home that they would avoid me. As I was walking in the back door they would be slipping out the front. They couldn't do anything right. I would see dishes in the sink and it would be enough to completely enrage me. Laundry baskets waiting to be taken downstairs, the lawn not mowed, or leaves not raked. Anything and nothing. I would tell them to get their rooms picked up or to do their homework. If they didn't clean their rooms I would go upstairs, throw a blanket on the floor and anything that was on the floor would be thrown on the blanket and put in the garbage. I don't mean put downstairs where they could get it back later. I took it to the dump and threw it out for good. Sometimes there were schoolbooks or new clothes. It didn't matter. Whatever it was was gone. I had no patience whatsoever. I didn't listen to what people said to me. I just told them what I wanted, and that was it, I expected it to be done. My wife and I would go shopping and every now and then I would get mad at a salesperson. I would very quietly tell my wife I was getting mad and that unless she wanted to be embarrassed she had better leave. After she left I would dress down the clerk and eventually the store manager. No one could approach me without taking their lives in their hands.

Then came the depression. I would get home and go right to bed. Five o'clock in the afternoon and I'd be in bed! I wasn't tired; it was just that if I were pretending to be asleep I would be left alone. I did not want to go anywhere or do anything. Pretty soon even my wife started to avoid me. No one would come over to visit because I was so rude. Eventually sleep wouldn't come at all. I had no interest in sex or even eating for that matter. After a year of this, I got a transfer to Niantic. Maybe things would be better there.

I managed to calm down for almost two years, but the seeds had been sown and eventually I started to get jumpy again. Only this time instead of being intolerant of inmates, it was staff. No one could do anything as good as I could. No one was as fast as I was. And of course no one saw things my way. Everyone had excuses, but I didn't bother to listen. My way was the right way and the only way.

I knew people were asking what had happened to me. Was I going through a divorce? Was I on drugs, or maybe drinking too much? When I entered a room, the conversation would change or stop altogether. I started to think that they were talking about me, when in fact people just stopped so that I wouldn't take part in the discussion and find fault with what they'd said. Pretty soon I couldn't find anyone to share lunch with. I took to eating in my car away from everyone. Eventually I started skipping lunch altogether; my stomach was acting up again.

Over the next couple of months it got worse. The other supervisors started to avoid me. All my reports were being questioned. It didn't matter what had happened or how, someone always had some comment to make or reason to reject it. It got to the point where I started to expect returned reports. It got so bad that I just didn't care. I would submit them with almost a sense of defiance. Almost hoping they would be rejected so that I could throw a temper tantrum. Pretty soon I was not reporting incidents or filing reports. And on some days I shredded reports when they were returned. I found myself doing all the things that I despised in others.

As if that wasn't enough, I started to question my own ability. I was so used to rejection that it became a way of life. My sex life went to shit and my bowels started acting up again.

This time it was worse. I went to the doctor and he told me that there was nothing wrong. I left thinking that he was incompetent. I couldn't sleep anymore. I would doze for an hour or so, then be wide-awake. I would get up in the middle of the night and watch television for a couple of hours. Then it was back to bed for an hour or so. Soon it would be time for work and I was already exhausted.

Nothing seemed to be working out right. I was in a bowling league, two actually, and my game went down the drain. I couldn't make tough shots anymore, the shots that the team depended on me to make. I just couldn't get it together anymore. I needed something to help me relax, but I refused to take anything so I started building lawn furniture.

This was supposed to give me some kind of release. I built some really fine stuff, and pretty soon it was in great demand. To me, every piece was a challenge. I needed to prove that I could do it. Who I wanted to prove it to I have no idea. I started doing harder and harder pieces. I needed to convince myself that I was good. I challenged those who bought my stuff to find anything wrong with it. Part of the challenge was that I never took a deposit. I would tell them that if it wasn't what they wanted when delivery time came then they didn't have to take it. I would brag that I always had someone else who wanted it. Most of the time I didn't. Sometimes stuff would sit in the yard for several weeks until someone wanted that particular piece. Sometimes when I couldn't find a buyer I would just give it away. I never let anyone know that they had stuck me for anything.

I couldn't share my feelings with anyone. Things were so bad at work that I couldn't bring myself to tell my wife. She didn't know anything about the job, so I figured she wouldn't understand. I just couldn't talk to anyone about it. I started sitting in the back yard all by myself. I took quite an interest in the local wild animals. Somehow I managed to tell them everything. They weren't much in the way of conversationalists but at least they couldn't find fault with me.

I guess that was when it really got bad. I couldn't function at all. I would listen to the radio and a song would come on that reminded me of something and it would get me upset or make me cry. Imagine, crying about something as stupid as a song. Even today I have no explanation for it. I know that I started thinking about suicide at that time. I just felt so lost, so empty. I think that's when I started getting close to the bottom. I was so wound up that all I wanted to do was get drunk and do something stupid so I could relax. The only problem with that idea was that I don't drink. I just wanted to laugh, but there wasn't anyone I could laugh with. There was no one I could trust. There was no one I could share my thoughts with. I couldn't control my emotions anymore and I think that if I had relaxed I would have just broken down and become a babbling idiot.

The bottom came one day without warning. I was working in my shop, or trying to work, and I found myself sitting in the dark and crying. I had my pistol in my hand. I don't know how it got there. There was no other way; I just couldn't bear being alone anymore. I had to relax. I just had to get some sleep.

I don't remember doing it, but I placed a call to John Nelson, the department's employee assistance program man. When he answered, I lost control and just broke down. I didn't know what to say. I tried to talk but couldn't. I just sat there and cried. He was very patient with me. I think he knew how close to the edge I really was. I managed to tell him I needed to talk. I pleaded with him to listen and eventually I told him everything.

That was three years ago and I'm still here. I owe John. I put my pistol away for over a year. I was afraid that if I carried it, I would use it. I'm seeing a therapist now and take

Prozac. I talk with my wife now. I have learned that I don't have anything to prove to anyone. I know what I am capable of. But that is what this job will do to you if you let it.

It takes its toll on all of us, each in different ways. It leads some to divorce, others to separation, drunkenness, drugs, or, maybe, therapy. If you're lucky enough to get through your career without any of this I envy you. I'll tell you this much; the odds are against you. Sooner or later the stress will have some effect on you. I just hope you have someone near you who can recognize the symptoms, someone you trust, someone you can talk to. Whether you talk to your spouse, significant other, doctor or clergyman, you have to share it with someone.

Best of luck to you.

Sally Walker

Every facility has maybe a half dozen really troublesome inmates who create problems every day. They don't care about discipline. They know that the courts awarded them a sentence and that they have to serve this sentence. They have resigned themselves to serving every single day of it. Most inmates try to stay out of trouble so that they can accumulate "good time."

For every week convicts behave themselves or maintain a job they can earn a day off their sentence. For these people the discipline process has meaning. If they get into trouble the system can take away some of their accumulated time. If they stay clean for six months, they can get it back. That is until they screw up and lose it again. For the troublemakers, the ones who have resigned themselves to making life miserable for everyone else, there is no good time to be taken or accumulated.

Troublesome inmates take a hell of a toll on staff, both physically and mentally . Driving to work I often feel that today is the day. Today I'll have to fight some inmate and someone is going to get hurt. I just hope it's not me. Sometimes I spend all day mentally preparing myself for combat. Every time the radio clicks my heart skips a beat. When the officer assigned to a violent inmate's unit calls for the lieutenant, my body releases a shot of adrenaline. The inevitable is coming. Just waiting for the call for assistance is killing me.

The smart inmates really know how to hurt staff, not just physically but emotionally. They like to wait until just before roll call or change of shift. Officers have been watching the clock. The day is almost done and there has not been a code. No one has been hurt and everyone is planning on getting out the door on time. Our guard is down; we've started to relax. "All available officers, Thompson seg, " or "code blue Thompson Hall." The whole day just went to shit!

All the good cops, the ones who really care are on their way to the call. The ones who are lazy or are just there for a paycheck pretend that they didn't hear the call. They usually get to their cars and slip out the back gate through Gates correctional. When they come in the next day they act so concerned that there was a code and someone got hurt. They pretend that had they heard the call they would have been there. It's really sad to think that they honestly think we believe them.

Sally Walker was a real piece of work. In the early 80s she decided she needed some attention and because she couldn't have a visit she wrapped herself in toilet paper and set it on fire. By the time staff got to her she had burns over most of her body. Even today she bears horrific scars on her torso and extremities.

Sally was doing time for possession, use and sales of drugs. That and child abuse. The state had her children. These kids were so traumatized that any communication between them and their mother had to be monitored. Once a month the state would bring them to see Sally, but most of the time the kids would make believe they were sick and unable to make the trip. Every now and then Sally managed to talk to them on the phone without someone listening in.

On these occasions she tried to get them to bring her drugs. Most of the time the kids would turn her in to the officials. When this happened the visit was canceled, Sally would throw a temper tantrum and a code would be called.

Sally was so bad that Niantic had to resort to a "one on one." A staff member was assigned to watch her twenty-four hours a day. When it first started Sally was just confined to her room and the officer sat out in the hall with the door open. This lasted maybe a week. Eventually Sally decided she wasn't going to stay in the room by herself, so the door had to be closed. When that got old, she would try to trash the room — smashing the bed, the window, the toilet, whatever. When this occurred we would have to restrain her, a code was called and she would be chained to the bed in a spread-eagle position.

After two or three hours, someone would take pity on her and order the removal of the restraints. Pretty soon this method had no effect as a deterrent. She decided about then that she was going to "cut up" or maybe "hang up" — slang for trying to hurt oneself. The responding staff would call medical, the nurses would clean her up and we would restrain her again. Only this time, because she was suicidal, we had to use soft restraints. After all, we didn't want her to hurt herself.

Soft restraints were designed for sedated or compliant inmates, not the likes of Sally Walker. On average, she could slip a set of soft restraints in about thirty minutes. Because of her history of assaulting staff, a code had to be called to put them back on. Eventually this too escalated, and Sally had to be restrained wearing only a paper gown. All this time she had to have a "one on one." And always Sally would verbally abuse the poor officer assigned.

Later Sally had to be housed in a strip cell — one with only a bed welded to the floor. Again this required a "one on one," and the inmate has no clothes, no gown, no nothing. When an inmate is housed in a strip cell only soft restraints can be used. The cell has a caged door through which the inmate can be observed. In Sally's case this worked for a little while as long as she was wearing restraints. Once they were removed she would throw feces and urine through the door at the staff. Then she would be restrained with soft restraints and hard restraints right over the top of the soft ones. She couldn't get out of these. All the years this was going on, Sally was housed in the mental health unit. But soon even they got tired of dealing with her so we moved her to the segregation unit. The mental health staff logic was that she was not a mental health problem she was a discipline problem. It took them almost six years to figure this out — fast thinkers they are not.

Now she was our problem. We didn't have to worry about some nurse standing over our shoulder whining about us hurting her. Sally was placed on the second floor of segregation in a room by herself. We figured now that she was away from the nurses she would realize we didn't want to play any more and settle down. Care to guess who was wrong on that one?

Sally maintained her disruptive behavior. She had to be restrained most of the time and was still abusive toward staff. One of the dumbest problems we faced in seg was that the doors were full wood doors and you couldn't observe the inmate when she was on a "one on one." There was a small six by eight window but you couldn't see the entire room. It was then that someone came up with the idea of what became known as the "fish bowl."

A new door was found that fit the opening and it was sent up to maintenance. A purchase order for Plexiglas was approved and the plan was set in motion. Two weeks later maintenance delivered the new door. It looked something like a full glass door except that on both sides Plexiglas was bolted together with security bolts. Each piece was three eighths of an inch thick with a one inch gap between them. Hell of a security door. Anyway, that worked. Sally could be observed by the one on one and still not throw anything at staff. There was a small slot on the bottom so that her food could be passed in. By the way, Sally didn't get a regular tray with regular food. Since she liked to throw things, we served her sandwiches and water. They were easier to clean up.

Inmates like Sally took a tremendous toll on the staff. I was sitting in the lieutenant's office with my only real friend, Sal Christaldi. He had come in a bit early to finish up the paperwork from the last fiasco with Sally Walker. I had just worked the night shift and we were talking about Sally when one of the deputy wardens came in to review the log. Sal held up a stack of papers to the Dep and mumbled, "Sally is a real piece of shit and a waste of time and energy. If half as much energy and time were spent on other things then this would be a great place to work."

He said he was just about fed up with Sally and the way she was acting. He went on to say that there were days when he just wished someone would take her out altogether, meaning shoot her or something. The Dep and I both nodded in agreement. I wasn't sure about the Dep, but the thought had crossed my mind a time or two.

A couple of hours later the major called Sal to his office. It seems that the Dep had told the warden about the conversation and she in turn decided that Sal was out of line. As a result of his comments the major had been directed to give Sal a formal counseling about his attitude towards the inmates and Sally Walker in particular. Sal couldn't believe it! We were just sitting talking. Kind of like wishful thinking. The kind where you hope you win the lottery. A counseling session! Unbelievable! An inmate can abuse staff, put them in the hospital or out on comp, set herself on fire, abuse her children, and destroy property and nothing happens to her. Yet a supervisor can make a make believe wish on a make believe star and get disciplined for it.

There is something wrong here.

Jane Doe

In the early 90's there was a consolidated effort in Connecticut as well as across the nation to prohibit abortions. Some of the protestors got arrested.

The department adheres to one policy: "We are here to hold you, not judge you. Whether you're right or wrong is none of our business."

Among the protestors was a smattering of religious people. Nice people, I guess, as long as your opinion wasn't contrary to theirs. Most of these people didn't identify themselves as clergy when they were arrested, for they felt that they should receive the same treatment as everyone else. This went right along with department policy which doesn't differentiate. If you're an inmate, you're an inmate. The rules are the same no matter what your occupation.

During one of these abortion clinic sit-ins in Hartford, the police decided to arrest the protestors. Buses were brought in and the collection made. When these people appeared before the judge most of them refused to cooperate. They refused to walk and had to be carried, refused to give their names, or even post the fifty-dollar token bond. Hence their arrival at Niantic.

We got somewhere between fifty and sixty women. The majority of them were middle-aged but there were some just out of their teens and a couple who qualified as senior citizens.

The Department of Corrections has strict guidelines concerning the processing of new admissions. Everyone, no matter who, must submit to the same process. This includes a strip search, medical check up, a shower (which included delousing), photograph, completion of an emergency contact sheet and an evaluation by the mental health department. The photographing process included holding a card under your face on which is written the name, inmate number, and date of birth.

Some of the protestors tried to clog up the system by refusing to give any pertinent information or completing the admissions process. This had no impact on the justice system whatsoever. They still received their inmate numbers but in place of a name we entered Jane Doe #1. The next one that refused was Jane Doe #2 and so on. A few thought it would be cute to refuse admissions altogether and among these were the clergy. When an inmate refuses admission, the process is halted and he or she is placed in a segregation area until they are ready to comply. Eventually they all give in but it takes about a week or so. A major tool in combating this type of behavior is not allowing them to have any contact with other inmates or visitors. Once they have complied with process then they received the same privileges as every one else.

Sometimes a priest would show up asking for someone by name and we would have to say that they weren't there. And in reality they weren't. A Jane Doe was, but not the person they were asking for. We didn't know who was who and for that matter we really didn't care. The court also had her as Jane Doe whatever and that was who we had.

The warden, an avid feminist, decided that since these women were not really criminals, we would not house them with the general population but rather in the gym. Sixty odd mattresses were brought in and placed on the floor. Now our gym was not like most high school gyms. We didn't have a shower area or bathroom. There was a bathroom but it was for only one person and was out in the hall. Also there was no place to brush your teeth or wash your face or take a shower. But that didn't matter to some of these people. I guess they figured that if they became disgusting enough we would eventually let them go. But ours is a waiting game, we have done this before and we possess great patience.

Everyday a driver would be assigned to transport eight of these women at a time over to the admissions area where there were showers and sinks. Those who wanted to could go, but it wasn't mandatory. After several days of sleeping on the floor in their clothes it became obvious that some weren't showering. The most shocking thing was the lack of interest in using the sanitation facilities. In an attempt to disrupt our routine, some of these inmates would defecate in the trashcans and just not tell anyone. Others would leave used sanitary napkins on the floor for someone else to pick up. I really felt sorry for the staff who had to work there.

We constantly received phone calls from family members inquiring about a relative who was last seen on the news being carried into a police bus. The general concern was about their health and if it was permitted to visit them. If we knew the inmate's right name we could usually be quite helpful. If the inmate insisted on remaining a Jane Doe then there was very little we could provide in the way of information to the families. We finally told the families to come down to the jail. When they got here we would have a stack of Jane Doe pictures and the family could pick out who they wanted. The family was then told that a visit wasn't possible because the admission process had not been completed. The families then usually provided the information we needed and a visit

88

was authorized. We in turn gave the information to the courts.

Every ten days or so the protestors were transported back to court to appear before the judge in an attempt to give them a chance to reconsider and post bond. Occasionally someone would post bond but very rarely. Even though they wouldn't answer to their real names, by the end of the third week we knew who everyone was. They were still under the impression that by not cooperating with us it was hurting the justice system. We just couldn't convince them that the courts didn't care if they posted bail or not. This wasn't bothering them all. The judges and clerks and sheriff's deputies went home every afternoon. They didn't care.

Eventually they all posted bond and went home, only to come back later when they refused to pay their token fine of fifty dollars. Then the process started all over again. Sometimes they would get arrested outside another clinic and try the same stuff. On these occasions, we just took out all the pictures from last time and tried to find a match. Sooner or later we would figure out who everybody was. The second time they would show up with all kinds of junk to make their stay a little more comfortable, only to have it confiscated during admissions. You would be amazed at what can fit in a body cavity.

We sometimes had problems with staff who were sympathetic to the cause. These officers would make phone calls for the inmates or carry out a letter and on some occasions bring items in. We never punished these people for their beliefs but for violating Department of Correction rules regarding conduct between inmates and staff. Once we figured out who the sympathetic staff were they were never assigned to that post again.

Sometimes one of the protestors would recognize a staff member who had transported an inmate to a clinic for a procedure. When that occurred the protestors would yell at the officer or throw things at her. We would then have to reassign that officer to another post. We didn't believe the staff had to be subjected to that kind of abuse.

Many of the other inmates felt we showed favoritism to the protestors. The common feeling was that they should be housed in general population. Most of the inmates support-ed the right to abortion and wanted a chance to confront the protestors on even terms. Knowing that such a meeting would turn physical, we never permitted such a meeting. To this day I don't think the protestors knew how lucky they were.

Code White

Every now and then the department gets hold of someone who turns out to be a real asset. I don't mean someone who ends up commissioner or anything like that; hell, an idiot can be commissioner, and we've already proven that several years ago in this state. This particular corrections officer did a fantastic job and the nurse did a lousy one. Some people are in the wrong profession and some are just incompetent.

Someone in the department decided that it would be nice if, when there was an emergency, we didn't panic the visitors. The result of this was a code system like the code system used by hospitals on television, but instead of dealing with a simple code blue when the shit hit the fan we had to get colorful.

Code orange: Officer needs assistance. All available officers. This means that if you are not directly involved supervising inmates you had better haul ass to the scene.

Code blue: A disturbance or riot. Again same as above. If you're not directly supervising inmates report to the scene.

Code red: Fire. All available officers get to the scene and lend assistance as needed.

Code green: Escape. If not directly supervising inmates, report to control. If you have a post, start locking down your unit and taking a count.

Code yellow: Hostage situation. You had better hope it isn't you. All available staff report to control for instructions.

Code white: Medical emergency. Designated medical staff report to the area with equipment. The primary driver or rover also report and the shift supervisor is to respond to all the codes.

It was a nice quiet Saturday at Niantic. As usual we were under-staffed and over-populated. That means about twenty officers and one lieutenant to about six hundred inmates. Hell of a ratio.

Niantic is situated on almost a thousand beautiful acres in southeastern Connecticut. It's almost like a college campus. Individual buildings built over fifty years ago are scattered here and there among the trees. Lead poured windows, hand carved banisters, solid oak doors, hardwood floors, just a perfect setting for the dregs of society.

The Fenwicks building was divided in half; one side for the teenyboppers, inmates under the age of twenty-one, and the other side for long-term inmates. I'm talking twenty years or more, but they have demonstrated they can behave themselves and hold regular jobs, some at the facility and some out in town. One of the nicer inmates living here was known as Miss Dolly.

I don't know what she did to get to Niantic, but then I really didn't care. I only know that she was like a housemother to the rest of the girls. She didn't have a real job because of her physical limitations. Being rather obese, requiring a cane to walk, she never left the building unless it was to go to medical or visits and then she needed a ride. None of the drivers ever minded picking her up to go somewhere and many a time if I was in the neighborhood I would take her in the supervisor's car.

There were two staff members assigned to Fenwicks South, the long-term unit. Mr. Connors came to us from the coast guard where he had been assigned to Alaska. Due to cutbacks, Connors was forced to leave early. His rate was that of corpsman, independent duty type, which means he was the cream of the crop, the best. (Independent duty corpsman are trained to work duty stations without a doctor and are trained to perform minor surgery and a whole lot of other great things.)

I got a call from Connors at maybe 9:00 or 9:30 in the morning. He told me he had an inmate who was sick and needed checking out. I told him to send her to medical, but when he called medical they told him to give her some Tylenol and tell her to lie down. Being a good officer, that is exactly what he did.

He called me again shortly after lunch and told me that the inmate was getting worse. He told me that he had called the nurse a second time and the nurse told him to leave it alone. Just give the inmate more Tylenol. I asked what he thought and he told me that he was concerned. He went on to say that it was Miss Dolly and she did not look good at all.

I went over and found Mr. Connors in the room with her. I motioned him to come to the office where we discussed what had already transpired. He told me that Miss Dolly needed to be in the medical unit — that in his opinion she was really sick. I went down to speak with her a moment and decided Connors was right. I told Miss Dolly I was going to get the nurse for her and that everything would be all right.

I got to medical a few minutes later and found the duty nurse sitting with the officer assigned to that area drinking a soda. I asked her if she had spoken with anyone from the Fenwicks concerning an inmate there. She said she had and that they were to give her some Tylenol and something to drink. I explained that it was Miss Dolly and that I was a little concerned. "After all, she never complains about anything and her condition today is out of the ordinary." The nurse told me that if Dolly came over to medical she would see her but not until.

"I don't think it's advisable to move her and I'd appreciate it if you could take a ride over and check her out."

She smiled and said, "The directive says that I'm not to leave medical unless there is a code white and until then I'm not going anywhere."

I turned to walk away but changed my mind. Right in front of the nurse I removed my radio from its case, keyed the mike and said, "Code white in Fenwicks south." I smiled at the nurse, put my radio away and said, "There is your code, now get your goddamn bag and get out to the car." She looked at me as if I were crazy and I told her to get her ass in gear, there's a code white.

On the way to the Fenwicks the nurse told me she didn't like my tone of voice or my attitude. She went on to say that it was her intention to notify her supervisor about this and write me up. I told her she could do whatever she damn well pleased but only after we settled Miss Dolly.

She examined Dolly, decided she was not well and needed to be in the medical unit for observation. I just looked at Connors and shook my head.

Just before shift change, the nurse called me and said Dolly needed to go to the emergency room. Somehow this didn't surprise me, but I said that I would find staff to go with her. It turned out Miss Dolly was admitted immediately to the cardiac unit, suffering a mild heart attack.

I called Connors. He mumbled something that sounded like I told you so. Hell of a way to run a jail!

I never found out if the nurse reported me or not. I know that no one ever spoke to me about it, so I guess not. Mr. Connors, by the way, gave up on custody and became a councilor.

The Liar

This is the story of a liar. I only had the chance to speak with this person on one occasion and then very briefly. I did not know all the facts at the time, so I took him at face value. I was to find out later that he had lied to the only person I trusted and to another whom I came to trust. He caused both of them many hours of unnecessary discomfort and concern for their own well being. Had any misfortune come to either of them, I promised I would see to it personally; it would not go unpunished.

It all started around the end of November, 1993. I had just reported to central office for my new assignment when we first met. Dunlap was around fifty. I thought he was retired military by the way he carried himself. Being ex- navy, I felt a kinship with him and was looking forward to having lunch so we could reminisce about the old days. I was confident the warden really knew what she was doing by surrounding herself with professional soldiers. This was going to be one hell of a team!

I had never had the opportunity to work a block with him and in retrospect I guess I was lucky. We were working out of central office to set up the Jennings Road Detention Center for Women. In addition to Warden Wilson were Captain Christaldi, maintenance officer Horace Smalls, and three lieutenants: Richard Carter, James Dunlap and myself.

To describe Mary Wilson is to describe an angel. That's what she is. She has to be. I have never met anyone who made me feel at peace the way she did. A tiny woman, when you were in her presence you had a feeling of awe. She had previously been a nun and why she ever chose corrections as a second occupation will forever be a mystery. That she will succeed at it is a certainty.

As a nun she worked as a volunteer at Hartford Correctional. The captain told me he remembered her from those days. He also told me she was just as charismatic then as she is now. When I first met her she was wearing two hats. She was the administrative assistant to the deputy commissioner as well as the warden of a new facility. Being an administrative assistant was a full time job, never mind trying to open a new jail. Imagine starting your own business from scratch. Trying to open a new facility requires about the same effort. On many a night I saw her take home another eight hours of work. She never went anywhere without her laptop and a mountain of directives or operational plans. Where she got the energy none of us ever knew.

Captain Salvatore Christaldi was my lifesaver. He had pulled me back from the brink and given me a second chance. When others tried to cast doubt he alone stood by me. Having worked the blocks in a hellhole called Big Cheshire, he had paid his dues. I took a tour of it once and that was enough for me. Six tiers back to back, stacked three high. Just the idea of working that alone took more guts than I've got.

I first met him when he got transferred to Niantic as a lieutenant. In the beginning, we worked third shift together. He finally got days as a unit manager and I stayed on third a while longer. When days were finally offered to me I jumped at the chance. (That was a choice I was later to regret). I should point out that being a couple of heterosexual males at a female facility automatically labeled us as trouble. The administration went out of its way trying to set Lt. Christaldi up. They gave him the two roughest units to manage. Not only did he do it but he did it damn well. Eventually the administration started to get to him like they did everyone else who wasn't female. On those days he would just go down to his unit and take care of business.

At that time a unit manager was responsible for an entire building. Anywhere from one hundred to one hundred fifty inmates plus staff. Somehow while being mother and father and confessor to the inmates and staff he managed to keep the warden off his back. That in itself was a feat I never learned.

Horace Smalls was a locksmith by trade. His business had gone under so he joined the state for lack of something better to do. His title was that of maintenance officer and having no motivation whatsoever, he had two basic speeds, slow and stop. Horace's goal was to make it to June. He would be vested by then and planned to move to Arizona. I don't know about the others, but I was counting the days.

Richard Carter and I never really got to know each other. He was split between New Haven Correctional and central office. New Haven didn't really want to turn him loose to us so he would work two days at central and three at the facility. I think that altogether we spent less than two weeks together. He wrecked his truck one day in bad weather while driving home and decided that the commute wasn't worth it. He eventually declined the position at Jennings Road much to everyone's regret. The warden had known exactly what she was doing when she recruited him because he knew his job and was really good at it.

James Dunlap was a mystery. How he ever kept things straight in his own mind was simply amazing. His credentials were impeccable. Ex military, Officers Corp, Viet Nam service (Purple Heart and Silver Star). He claimed to have worked as an intelligence specialist for an unnamed agency out of Langley, Virginia. He also boasted of having friends in another investigative agency located in Washington.

Dunlap was a lieutenant at the Garner Correctional Facility when it went off. That is a term used by corrections staff to refer to a riot or major disturbance. In this case it was a riot. Although the facility itself suffered considerable damage, the biggest loss to the department was in the way of careers. A lot of good staff went down on that one.

After Garner was back under control and order had been restored, the commissioner toured the facility. Upon hearing from several inmates reports of excessive force, he ordered an investigation into the allegations. A fair amount of information and documentation was collected through videotapes shot during the incident. The film substantiated the allegations of excessive force. Another source of information came from staff who ratted on other staff. This is called dropping dimes. Anyone who drops dimes is not well thought of by either staff or inmates. If it's an inmate, there is a real good chance that when he's caught he's going to end up in the emergency room. If it's staff he can expect to get beat down in the parking lot after work.

Anyway, it seems that Lt. Dunlap claimed he had witnessed several incidents of excessive force — incidents that were graphically detailed in his statement to internal affairs. His statement was so detailed that I heard it was over ten pages long. Now that's not bad for someone who was on the other side of the jail when the shit hit the fan. There had always been some doubt as to whether he responded to the call for assistance or not. I never heard of anyone seeing him in the conflict but that's not to say that he wasn't there. I'm just thinking that maybe he got there after things were under control and order had been restored.

As a result of Dunlap's statement, several supervisors

were placed on administrative leave, demoted, transferred or just plain fired. At the commissioner's request, the tapes and statements were made available to the attorney general's office. They in turn pursued criminal charges against staff. On the other side of the coin, the inmates got lawyers and lawsuits became the order of the day.

The commissioner personally called Dunlap to his office and commended him for his honesty and integrity. Dunlap also received some kind of commendation. In the commissioner's opinion Dunlap was a perfect example of who we should be promoting to managerial positions.

Now being a dime dropper, Dunlap could not return to the Garner Correctional Facility, hence his assignment to the Jennings Road Detention Center. The logic was that he would be close to central office where he could be watched over by the administration and groomed for advancement. Great things awaited James Dunlap.

I was selected for Jennings Road by the captain. He knew I needed to get out of Niantic and this was the perfect opportunity. The problem was that the warden at Niantic had called Warden Wilson and told her that I had suffered a nervous breakdown earlier that year. She went on to say that I was a little unstable and advised against taking me on (I didn't crack up and it was never documented by Niantic that I had a problem). It took a little convincing on the captain's part but Warden Wilson agreed to give me a chance. (I have always wondered if she ever regretted that.)

I think it was on my third day at central office that I heard Lt. Dunlap had been arrested for second-degree aggravated assault. It seems he had a little misunderstanding with his ex-wife and went after her with a bayonet attached to a rifle. Somebody called the cops and Dunlap got arrested. Out of what could be referred to as professional courtesy, they later released him on a promise to appear.

The next day he did what we are all told to do if we get into trouble with the law and that is to notify the warden. The warden in turn called the captain and the three of them had a closed-door meeting. When they finished, the captain agreed to drive Dunlap to his apartment to get cleaned up.

The captain told me later that as they arrived at Dunlap's place, he noticed Dunlap's car was parked on the other side of the apartment complex. He mentioned this but received no comprehensible reply.

As they entered the apartment the smell made the captain almost sick to his stomach. He said that there was trash everywhere. Dirty dishes were piled sky high in the sink and on the counters. Uniforms and clothes were strewn about in every room. It was about then that Dunlap commented on the captain's POW bracelet. (The captain had also served in Viet Nam in the early seventies. He wore this bracelet constantly. On it was the name of someone who had been taken prisoner and as yet had not returned home. Only when he did, would it be removed and sent to him. It was a way of saying he would never be forgotten.) When Dunlap started talking about the bracelet he gave the captain the impression that he hadn't known the story behind it.

Dunlap said that he too had been in Viet Nam. He told the captain that he had served as a helicopter pilot and had been shot down. He went on to say that he had been captured and in the end released. Inquiring as to his rank, the captain was surprised to hear that Dunlap had been a warrant officer in the air force. This surprised the captain because the air force hadn't flown helicopters in Nam. About then Dunlap proudly pulled from a drawer a set of what he claimed were his shoulder boards. They weren't air force and they weren't that of a warrant officer. Rather than risk an argument the captain said nothing.

Dunlap rambled on for awhile, then seemed to change. He

became very agitated about his arrest and pulled out a bayonet. He said that this was what his wife had tried to cut him
with and he wasn't going to stand for it. About now, the captain was starting to get a little nervous. Dunlap told him he
was not someone to be taken lightly, that if anyone messed
with him he would fuck them up. The captain just nodded in
agreement.

Somehow the conversation got around to guns and
Dunlap asked the captain for a small favor. It seemed Dunlap
was concerned someone might break into his apartment and
steal his pistols. What he wanted the captain to do was to
store them for a few days at his house. Captain Christaldi
said that he really wasn't comfortable keeping them but finally gave in when Dunlap explained that the guns were all disassembled and inoperable.

Dunlap produced a box full of several World War II German
Lugers. He told Christaldi that they had been taken from
POWs at the end of World War II and were very valuable. The
box was placed in the captain's car. As the two of them were
leaving for central office the captain saw Dunlap slip the bayonet into the box. The captain didn't say anything at the time
but he was definitely rattled.

As soon as they arrived at central office the captain and
the warden had another closed-door meeting, this time without Dunlap. The captain told the warden about the box and
between the two of them they decided to call the police
department for advice. It was about the same time that the
police were trying to call them. They had a warrant for
Dunlap and wanted to know where he was. It was agreed that
the captain would bring Dunlap down to the station after
lunch. The warden told the cops about the box and a cruiser
was dispatched immediately to collect it.

The captain drove Dunlap to the police station where an
arrest was made and bond set at ten thousand dollars.

Captain Christaldi told Dunlap about giving up the box. Dunlap went ballistic, saying that he had been sold out by the warden and captain. He reiterated he should not be messed with and that he would get even with anyone who fucked with him. The captain believed him.

A bondsman had been called and the wheels set in motion. Now it seemed that the bondsman and the captain knew each other and the bondsman told the captain that he really didn't want to post the bond but would as a favor. (It had been agreed between the warden and the captain that they would stick by Dunlap, as he was part of our team.) Reluctantly the bondsman continued processing the bond. The bondsman went on to say that he knew of Dunlap from other incidents and that there was more to the man than either the warden or captain realized.

The bondsman told them that when he ran Dunlap through the computer there were several discrepancies in what Dunlap said and what the federal government said. It was based on this that the bondsman was hesitant. Dunlap asked the captain if he could help him with the putting up ten per cent cash required for the bond and the captain passed, claiming he didn't have that kind of cash on him. It turned out that Dunlap posted the ten percent from money he had on him when he was arrested. It was about now that the captain figured out Dunlap was trying to con him and the warden. This really pissed him off but he managed to hold his tongue. It was then that I became involved.

The captain told me he was very concerned about the warden. Dunlap had included her in his ravings and so we started staying a little late waiting for the warden. We used the excuse that we were staying just to make sure her car started in the cold or that we just wanted to help her carry all her stuff out. We didn't want her slipping on the ice. I know there were a couple of nights that the captain followed her home. He never knew it but there were also a couple that I followed him.

Based on what the warden told the commissioner, Lt. Dunlap was placed on administrative leave pending investigation. This ended up taking about six weeks. One day the warden asked me if I could bring a couple of metal detectors to her office. It turned out that internal affairs wanted to have a talk with Dunlap but they wanted to make sure he wasn't carrying anything when they did. That everyone was concerned would be stating it mildly. Internal affairs never wore their weapons in central office yet whenever Dunlap was scheduled to appear they were all carrying.

As it turned out the only thing the department could get Dunlap for was lying. He was fired for lying on his employment application when he stated that he had been honorably discharged.

As for the staff at Garner, some of the people in trouble because of Dunlap's statements filed grievances to get their jobs back. What became of them I have no idea. Dunlap also hired a lawyer and filed to get his job back. About six months ago I had a chance to speak with the attorney who represented him. It seems that someone in personnel had messed up on the paperwork and the department had not followed proper procedure. As a result, Dunlap was reinstated. He received all his back pay and time. Since Dunlap was now an embarrassment to the department, they offered to let him resign without prejudice. In the end, he was allowed to leave with a disability pension for stress.

That was a couple of years ago. No one has seen Dunlap since then, but that's not to say he's been forgotten.

I still remember my promise.

The Great
Key Fiasco

There was a new warden at Jennings Road, where I was now working with Captain Christaldi, Horace Smalls, maintenance officer, Lt. Morris Potter and myself. With only five people, all of them supervisors, you would think we wouldn't screw up. Hey, the world isn't perfect.

The Jennings Road facility used to be the city's lock up. The police department closed it down due to budget cutbacks; then the state leased the space from the city of Hartford. The politicians were goofing off as usual, so we didn't have a lease for the building and we weren't really supposed to be in there. The city of Hartford and the police department were nice to allow us in to set the place up for its eventual opening.

Every morning we would stop by the police station and pick up the keys to the building. Once it was unlocked we would return the keys. The only problem with this system was that the business manager had the keys, and she was quite possessive. We'd have to wait for her to come in, then pick up the keys and return them directly to her. This also meant that if she wasn't in or hadn't made other arrangements, we couldn't get into the building. We didn't need the keys at the end of the day to lock up because there were electric doors. When it was time to leave we just closed all the doors and left.

Some days we'd take off early. Potter or I would stay until after four, then close up. On this particular Friday, Potter was doing something on the computer, so he volunteered to stay. The captain had something planned for the evening, The warden was going to the casino, and I was going to a local theater to see a Kathy Mattea concert with my wife. The day went down the drain at about ten minutes to seven.

We were just heading out the door when the phone rang. My wife answered and said it was Lt. Potter. She had that "not again" look on her face, but I smiled and told her nothing was going to screw up the night we'd planned. Morris told me he had a small problem. "I'm locked out of the jail."

"Locked out? How the hell did you do that?"

"I stepped outside to get something out of my car and the door slammed behind me."

"Hey, it's late. Just go home."

"I thought about that, but I can't. Everything inside is still open."

"Everything? What do you mean by everything?" I asked.

"Everything," he repeated. "Control, the inner Sallyport door (a security entrance consisting of two doors, an inner and an outer — one of which is kept locked at all times), the office doors, the coffee pot and the lights are still on, and the computers, too."

I couldn't believe it. I asked him what he was still doing there at seven o'clock, and he said that this had happened at about four-thirty and he was still trying to figure out what to do. I told him there wasn't much he could do but call the captain. "I'm on my way out the door."

"I did, " Lt. Potter said, "and the captain told me to call the warden."

As soon as I heard that I knew we were in deep shit. The warden was the kind of person who didn't believe in accidents. According to him, he had never made a mistake and didn't think others should either. According to him, he was the only one in this jail who knew what he was doing, and it was only due to his great patience that he tolerated the rest of us.

"Call the warden?" Disregarding the ass chewing we were going to get, there was a reason for the captain's logic. The warden had decided he should have keys to everything. That included the front doors. He'd reasoned that if he wanted to work on weekends he'd be able to just let himself in.

The captain, Morris and myself had advised him against that. We told him that there was a control officer for that. He said "What if the control officer isn't there?"

We pointed out that it would never happen because control is never left unmanned.

He was persistent. He went on to say that maybe there was a time when he might want to sneak in so that he could check up on staff. Again, that was never going to happen because of the control officer. For his every argument, we had the correct response. It finally came down to the fact that the building wasn't ours, it belonged to the city. He said that if they didn't know, then it wouldn't matter.

I remember the captain asking where this key would be kept? The warden said at his condo. We pointed out to him that the department had very strict guidelines as to where and how keys should be stored. He said he would take care of it and that the discussion was closed.

For several days thereafter the discussion raged on between the captain, Potter and myself, all in vain. The warden had already told Mr. Smalls to get him a set of keys to the front doors. I just couldn't believe it. An unaccountable set of keys. Keys not on the inventory. Unheard of, to say the least. We are not talking about a regular set of keys here. The main key was a Folger Adams, which had to be special ordered from the company. The second was a special security key with beveled cuts that prohibit tampering. Again, a special order.

It turned out that the warden didn't keep them secure at his condo but kept them in the glove compartment of his car. Such stupidity would normally get someone fired, but we were directed not to mention the keys to anyone, and we didn't.

Morris Potter was a new lieutenant and was still a little unsure of himself. I had told him right from the beginning to call me if he ever had a problem. "Most things can be handled discreetly if you act fast enough." Now I told him I would page the warden and see what he wanted to do. First I called the captain to see if Potter had really spoken to him. He wasn't at home so I left a message to call or page me. Then I paged the warden. By now it was 7:15, and my wife was starting to get a little upset.

The warden called me shortly. "Are you sitting down?" I asked.

"No, but tell me anyway."

"Potter's locked out, " I said.

"OK, so what? It's after seven and he shouldn't be in there anyway."

That's when I told him about the building not being secure. Surprisingly he wasn't as mad as I thought he was going to be. "Where's Potter now?"

"He's there trying to find a way in."

"Why did he call you instead of the captain, and where did he call from?"

"The police station. Then he went right back to the jail." I asked the warden if there was a chance he could stop by the jail with his key, but that was out of the question because he was in Ledyard, forty miles away. He told me he had to think a minute and would call me right back. By now my wife was really getting mad.

107

Inside of five minutes, the warden called back and said that if he had his way he'd leave Potter there all weekend watching the building. I told him we really couldn't do that unless he wanted to pay Potter for the time. "Pay him? Under no circumstances! It's his screw up, so let him suffer."

I let him vent. Finally, the warden agreed to meet me in Norwich. I'd get his key, drive back to Hartford, check the place out and then lock up.

My wife was ripping mad. What about the show? I told her she would have to go alone, or maybe with her sister. The tickets had been a surprise for me and she had been looking forward to the concert for weeks. I told her I knew, but under the circumstances the jail came first. As it was, she took her sister, but not without first directing a few barbs at Potter, the warden and myself.

The little trip to get the keys was going to take some time. It was, after all, twenty-five miles to Norwich, then forty to Hartford and fifteen back to my house. This was going to be a long evening. On my way to Norwich, the captain called me in the truck. I told him where we stood and what I was doing. He agreed with the plan, saying that he really couldn't have done anything different. I went on to tell him what the warden had said about Potter and the weekend.

That's when he told me that Potter had called him at around five o'clock to inform him what had happened and that he had called him from home!

"Are you sure he was home?" I asked. The captain was sure, because he had heard Potter's wife talking to him in the background. This meant that Potter had lied to me. After speaking with the captain, Potter decided to go back to the jail and make like he'd never left. He then called me, hoping I would think of a way out of the mess.

When I got to Norwich, the warden was steaming. He made several ethnic remarks about Potter but I pretended not to hear. He told me he wanted Potter's ass for this; that I was to make sure Potter understood that come Monday morning when he came in, there had better be a report on his desk. I told him I would make sure Potter knew.

I got to the jail at about eight-thirty and found Potter in the police station talking with the desk officer. We went around to the jail and Potter asked what the warden had said.

"You don't really want to know." I said. "The warden is really pissed at you and expects a report Monday." Potter was a little rattled, and for good reason. The police department had reached the business manager and she was on her way in to get us the keys.

Decision time. There I was with an unauthorized set of keys. If we locked up before she got there, she'd know we had a set. Our only choice was to sit and wait for her. Just before nine she arrived, and I could tell the moment she stepped out of her car that she was not a happy camper. I apologized for the inconvenience and just stood there with head held low while she had a piece of my ass regarding our incompetence. Potter in the meantime was cowering over by the door. When I returned with the key he asked if she was upset. Just a little, I told him. I offered to let him give her back the keys but he declined. When I returned them, I lost another bit of ass.

Potter and I entered the building and conducted a security check. Everything was as it should be. We turned everything off and secured the building. Out in the parking lot we had a little talk.

I told him again that the warden was really pissed off and asked him exactly what had happened, pointedly asking if he had left the area. He told me only to use the phone at the police station. I said nothing. The problem was that I had assured the warden Potter had been there all the time and now I was in it and part of the lie.

Just before we started home, Potter asked what he should put in the report. I told him I really didn't know, that I had a very upset wife, and I was trying to figure out how to deal with that. Because of him I had missed what was to have been a really great concert. He apologized to me but I knew he really didn't mean it. We decided that tomorrow night he should call me at home. By then I would have figured this out.

On my way home I called the captain, briefed him on what had happened and told him I would help Potter with the report. I went on to say I would make sure that he had a copy before the warden got it. It was now 9:45.

Saturday night Potter called me and for over two hours we prepared the report. Everything in it was correct except for Potter going home. Somehow that fact was left out. Come Monday morning, everyone had a copy.

When the warden came in, Potter was discreetly indisposed. First the captain and the warden talked behind closed doors. Then it was Potter's turn. While that was going on, the captain and I talked. He told me the warden had said he was going to have Potter's ass on this one.

"He's mad at me, too, for not coming for the keys. He said you acted like a captain should in a crisis. I should have been the one checking out the building and chewing Potter out."

I apologized for getting him in trouble but at the time my way was faster as I was closer. The captain couldn't have done anything different. It was a simple incident and I had everything under control. The captain said he understood.

After lunch it was my turn with the warden. He asked me what had happened when I got to the jail with the keys. I explained that knowing the business manager was on her way in, I elected to keep our keys a secret. "Smart choice, " he said.

Nothing ever came of this. Potter didn't get hammered.

The captain and I just went about our business. The unauthorized keys? Well the police department never found out and the warden probably still has them. The captain transferred out and a while later I was forcibly transferred. They said I wasn't a team player. My wife kept me in the doghouse for several weeks. Whenever she could, she would comment on the show saying how wonderful it had been. I'm convinced Kathy Mattea puts on a great show, and I hope some day to see her.

Sometimes I really hate this job.

Dirty Cops

I had been at the Jennings Road Detention Center for about six months, but we still weren't open yet. We were supposed to have opened in January of 1994, but because of budget constraints and political inactivity it was July before we even got some staff.

The staff was supposed to arrive on Friday and we were getting inmates on Monday. Aside from not having rosters set up, no medical coverage, no sanitation, and no food, we were in great shape.

The warden was more paranoid about it than I was. Sam was a product of the system. The way the system works, if you have someone incompetent working for you and you want to get rid of them, you promote them. Sam had come into the system as a counselor's aide and ended up in training somehow. Imagine a training officer who had never worn a uniform or worked a block being responsible for teaching new staff. Our standard joke was that the only way Sam could tell the difference between staff and inmates was staff had to wear uniforms. I never spoke to anyone who ever saw him in a housing unit. What qualified him for a warden's job I have no idea.

That he was afraid of inmates was obvious from the beginning. What made it worse was that he was also afraid of women. That really qualified him for this job. To him they were ladies and should be treated that way. Hell, half the inmates couldn't spell lady let alone think they might be one.

Captain Sal Christaldi was one of the best. He knew how to get the most out of his people. And with over twenty years in the department, there was never a doubt that he knew what he was doing. He had worked some of the roughest facilities in the state and had seen things some people only dream of. He never let you down and you were always sure of where you stood with him. Unlike most people of that time who changed attitudes or positions depending on who was in power or favor, Captain Christaldi was a fantastic constant.

I was his "chief dog robber." That's an army term, usually used with respect. If he needed something, I got it and he knew not to ask where it came from. That he was a clean freak was obvious. He would tell you right from the beginning if you wanted to stay on his good side, the place better be clean. I used to joke with him. "You want it clean, you clean it. You want something fixed, get out of the way." We were a hell of a team. He knew how to work the system and I knew how to work.

I think the warden was jealous. The captain had friends in places that the warden only dreamed of. I often heard the warden tell him that if we wanted something we would have to go through channels. The captain would make a phone call and we would have it that day. It wasn't meant to be insubordination; it was just a way of getting things done. My job was to know who had what and where it was. The captain had the names of who to call.

Jennings Road consisted of cellblocks only and was originally used by the police department as a holding unit. Designed as a level five facility, it shared the building with the police department. A level five designation means that it could hold maximum-security inmates. Originally designed to hold 114 inmates in its heyday, it held 200 on average.

There were fifty-seven cells — each designed to hold two inmates. The beds were bunk style welded to the walls. The cells were eight feet long and six feet wide. Each had a stainless steel toilet and sink combination. The doors were all electric, opened and closed by the control officer who was located in another part of the jail. The block officer had to call control on the radio or telephone to tell which door he wanted opened or closed. Video cameras were mounted in the ceilings to help monitor the blocks.

There were four cellblocks — A, B, C, D. "A" block consisted of the officer's station and twenty-four cells, twelve on each side of the tier. "B" block had twenty-five cells and a common shower area. The same officer was responsible for both tiers. The previous administration got away with it being a one-officer post by not allowing the inmates out except for showers or medical reasons and then only two at a time. On the other hand, Sam didn't think the girls needed to be in cells, so at any given time there were twenty to thirty inmates out running around socializing.

"C" and "D" blocks were on the other side of the jail. These were meant to be for those inmates who cleaned during the day, did the inmate laundry, or served the meals when and if they arrived. What we did was use "D" block for the workers and "C" block as a segregation or punishment unit. "D" block had its own shower and television. It was used as an incentive for the workers. "C" didn't have anything. If inmates in seg needed to take a shower they were escorted to the admissions area and permitted to use that shower.

"A" and "B" had to share a common TV mounted in the day room, a room that measured just twelve by twenty feet. Not a lot of room for ninety-eight inmates. The day room also doubled as the serving area for meals.

The original plan, way back when, was that we would house Niantic's problem children. They were going to spend all their time in cells with only very limited time out. There would be no contact visits. A large reinforced lexan partition separated inmates from visitors and any conversation was over a sound powered telephone. This way we could control incoming contraband.

We had anticipated all potential problems from cell confinement to sexual activities to inexperienced staff. What we didn't anticipate were dirty cops.

The inmates are very experienced at recognizing weaknesses in staff. The captain and I spent many hours trying to explain the pitfalls of working with female inmates. In most cases we were a success but some always slip by the wayside. All we could hope for was that we would see it coming and be able to intervene in time.

I don't know the exact approach the inmates used. We had taught staff about how inmates will play the officer's ego, expose themselves to staff, use simple flattery, sympathy, tears, and misunderstanding. Techniques were directed not only at the male staff but the women also. Women are just as susceptible to subtle seduction as men.

In this case, the targets were three male officers, one on second shift and two on third. I won't mention their names, but maybe they'll get caught for something. I sure hope so.

One day I received a note from an inmate telling me that some of the girls were going outside on third shift to smoke and joke with the officers. This was definitely against the rules. No outside doors were to be opened during the night except in an emergency. What they were doing was opening the fire escape doors at the end of the tier after the lieutenant had made his rounds. The note also mentioned the use of drugs. I discreetly approached the writer of the note and voiced my concern. The informant told me that in exchange

115

for cigarettes and drugs, the girls were having oral sex with the officers. She went on to tell me that the girls involved were bragging they could get whatever they wanted. All they had to do was ask, and their man would bring it in.

By now the captain had been transferred, so I was on my own. After a couple of weeks I felt I had enough information to present my case to the warden. He didn't believe me. Later I learned he too had been smitten by one of the ringleaders and just couldn't imagine how such a sweet young thing could do something like that. He told me that unless I caught them in the act I was to drop it. I told him in order to catch them I was going to need some help but he told me I was going to have to do this on my own. I thought about it for a couple of days and just couldn't let it go.

I carefully prepared a letter to the head of the security division. I mentioned everything, the sex, the drugs, flowers, cards, all of it. I went on to say that my informant even knew where the drugs were being hidden when they came in. My informant would also tell me in advance when the next shipment was coming in, who was bringing it, and when the transfer would be made. I included a map of the facility showing where they were going for smokes and sex and approximately what time of night.

I mentioned that several officers were involved and that they had to work together because the cell doors could only be opened by the control officer and that it was his job to keep tabs on the lieutenant. I called the head of security and told him I was faxing this package over to him and him alone. I didn't trust anyone else.

I think the warden and the security chief got together, because nothing came of my letter or call. I did detect a change in attitude towards me by staff and the warden. I think the warden snitched me out. Little did I know that my days at Jennings Road were numbered.

I kept track of what was happening. The drugs and sex got more obvious. It was almost as if they felt they were immune to being caught. In a way I guess they were. All I can do now is shake my head in disgust. They say what goes around comes around. I sure hope they're right.

A Team Player

It was October of 1994, and I thought my big chance had arrived. Captain Christaldi had transferred to the Corrigan facility and his slot at Jennings Road was now vacant. I had been waiting for this for a long time. I had stayed out of trouble, kept my mouth shut and tried to do everything a captain was supposed to do. Captain Christaldi had spent many weeks trying to groom me for the slot and we both felt I was ready.

Captain Christaldi had started my training even before the vacancy had occurred. He assigned most of the duties a captain would normally do for a new facility to me, such as the post assignments and rotations for the staff. This entailed balancing each shift with females and minorities. I scheduled all vacation requests and slotted coverage when one of the other lieutenants wanted time off.

One of my normal collateral duties was that of purchasing officer. The only reason I got that job was because no one else wanted it. That and maintaining the supply inventories. I also took care of our meals, transportation requirements, and approval or scheduling of all maintenance requests. All this and shift supervisor, too.

When we first opened, there were only two experienced lieutenants and the captain. Our first month was spent working twelve-hour shifts training the new lieutenants and just being around to offer guidance. It was fun but it sure played hell with my home life. Because of my collateral duties, I assigned myself to work from 4:00 a.m. till 4:00 p.m. Do that six days a week and it makes for a lot of short nights and long days!

Anyway, the interviews were all scheduled and it was just a matter of waiting. I had been through this before so I had some idea of what to expect. There were the usual phone calls from my friends asking if I would be upset if they came down for a try. I had done the same thing at other facilities, so I was happy they thought well of me and I told them I welcomed the challenge.

About fifteen people were interviewed, but I was confident that I was the front runner. After all, not only was this my facility, but I had also served as acting captain on several occasions during the past year. I was surprised to find out that it took qualifications other than knowledge to get the job.

The lady from personnel arrived right on time and as usual the warden was late, so we killed some time over coffee. She and I had spent many hours together interviewing lieutenants, and we got along pretty well. I asked if I could see the list of applicants and was surprised to see that the last name on the list was the warden's girlfriend. I pointed out that she had only been a lieutenant for ten months and was not on the approved captain's list. The personnel lady said she would check it out.

The second day of interviews started with a bang. The personnel lady told the warden that his friend wasn't eligible for the position. I heard later that the warden had very abruptly told her he would interview whomever he liked. Needless to say, his girlfriend got the job. I'm not sure what her qualifications were but I have a good idea.

119

About a week after she got the job, I received a note from the warden saying that we were getting some new staff and to slot them. I was still a little mad, so I forwarded it to the captain with a note attached telling her that it is usually the captain's job to slot new staff. She in turn took the note to the warden.

A day later I was called to his office. He wanted to discuss his note as well as mine. He asked why I hadn't complied and I politely told him that normally the captain does things like that. He pointed out that he had sent the job to me, not the captain. I smiled and said that since he had never worn a uniform or worked a block I figured he didn't know who was supposed to do what. He was adamant; he wanted me to do it. I again pointed out that it was the captain's job and that I would defer to her. After all, she was privy to the warden's wishes regarding staff assignments. I went on to say that it wasn't my problem that she didn't know how to do it. If she were as qualified as he thought she was for the job, then she would know how to do it.

At this point the conversation got ugly. The warden closed the door and wanted to know where we stood. I just couldn't pass that by. After a little ass chewing, he asked me what my relationship with the captain was. I pointed out that we weren't having a relationship, since I was married and so was the captain. He hit the roof. He asked if I had any problem working for the captain. "No, " I said. "I'll give her all the respect that her bars entitle her to." Not being able to let things alone, I went on to point out that I had the utmost confidence in her ability. "No one can play solitaire on the computer as well as she can." Then I left.

After two days of brainstorming behind closed doors, the captain ended up calling her husband who was a major at another facility and he slotted the new people. I could have done it in thirty minutes, but that was a subject none of the other lieutenants wanted to bring up outside our office.

At about this time the department instituted its smoke free policy. We had been cutting back over the last several weeks but now it was official. There would be no smoking whatsoever inside the facility. This wasn't a big problem for the staff and inmates, as most had already quit smoking. The exceptions were the warden, the captain, and two lieutenants. None of them felt the rules applied to them.

That was like a red flag to a bull. To me, the rules apply to everyone. Whenever I found an ashtray, rather than ignore it, I would throw it away. I didn't feel that I should have to clean up after them or be subjected to working in their mess. After about a week of this I wrote the warden and let him know that this was a smoke free facility and that I took exception to the staff smoking inside. It wasn't my intention to be a stickler for the rules; I just wanted to mess with him and the captain.

I decided to write to the region administrator protesting the captain's promotion. I pointed out that she only had ten months as a lieutenant and wasn't eligible to be interviewed, not having met the minimum requirements. When he didn't reply, I decided to write the commissioner. Again nothing.

I was more than a little surprised to hear from the personnel lady, though. She called me at home and told me that I had just been transferred to another facility. She told me that there was no need for me to return to Jennings Road and that she would take care of my check and time and attendance records. She told me that the warden and his girlfriend pitched a bitch to the director, saying that I wasn't a team player. She went on to tell me that I was to report to the warden of my new facility at 9:00 a.m. the following day.

When I reported to work , I was surprised to find out that no one knew I was coming. The warden had to call personnel to find out what was going on. No one had even bothered to tell him I was reporting. It was then that I decided to get a lawyer.

I filed a complaint alleging reverse discrimination and violation of state hiring guidelines. Unfortunately, I retained an idiot lawyer and lost the complaint along with a couple of thousand dollars. I was also up for the major's exam but was so bummed out about the Jennings Road fiasco that I canceled my oral exam. I just couldn't concentrate on something of that magnitude. Because of what happened at Jennings Road, I probably wouldn't have got a passing grade anyway.

But a couple of good things did come out of all this. The captain ended up getting demoted and the warden was relieved. When Jennings Road closed, the ex-captain ended up across the state at another facility and has yet to be interviewed for another promotion. There was no spot for the warden, so he took a demotion to deputy warden at another facility. He pulled something stupid there and ended up getting demoted a second time and transferred again. I hear he is not well thought of at his new job and is referred to as the lounge lizard. They say he is afraid of the inmates. I can believe that.

That was almost two years ago. Since then I have been labeled as a troublemaker and have never received another serious interview. The captain's exam is coming up again and this time around I don't think I shall even apply. I see no reason to give them a chance to bad mouth me again. Maybe, just maybe, someday someone will need a supervisor who really can do the job and I'll get a phone call. But I'm not holding my breath.

The Man in the Can

Inmates have a way of coming up with some rather colorful expressions. I guess when all you have to do all day is watch your keepers, you get a little inventive. I think the best one is "the man in the can." An assaultive inmate told me, "I would've beat that correction officer's ass if it weren't for that other son of a bitch." Another said, "The lieutenant cheated. I could have beaten them but that goddamn lieutenant sprayed me."

Over the last couple of years, the department has realized that to win in confrontational situations you have to have an edge. In our case that edge is Capstun. The days of piling on an inmate or beating him down are over. People get hurt when you do that and most of the time it's the staff. We are bound by rules about what we can do and where we can strike. Inmates aren't. They bite, scratch, kick, punch, gouge — anything to win.

Capstun is a chemical irritant spray. It is not mace or the product sold in stores called pepper mace. It is an oleoresin extract of capsicum pepper. All natural, it does not do any permanent damage and dissipates naturally in about forty-five minutes. It doesn't inhibit breathing and has no adverse effects on asthma sufferers but sure does whip a hurting on the eyes and mucus membranes. When someone is sprayed with it, the natural reaction is to try to back away throwing the hands up to protect the eyes. Fortunately for staff, the reaction to the spray is instantaneous.

Clean up is a department requirement. After the inmate is sprayed and restrained he or she must be given the opportunity to clean up. This consists of a change of clothes, a shower, and medical attention if deemed necessary. It is recommended that when taking a shower you approach the spray from behind and let the residue wash away from the face. If you don't, there is the possibility that the water will only carry the spray from your hair back into the affected areas. Finally, the supervisor has to complete the proper paperwork indicating the use of chemical agents and why.

I've been in fights where we've won and in some where we've lost. Actually, we never lose. We may suffer a setback and have to get more staff or wait until a later time when we know the inmate is alone, but we will eventually win. The goal is to do so without getting hurt. I have had teeth knocked out and glasses broken; I have been cut, gouged, kicked and just plain beat on and I have found that the older I get the longer it takes for me to recover. So now I avoid the physical stuff whenever I can. My philosophy is: "You fight, I'll watch."

I have learned over the years, either from experience or listening to people I respect, that discretion is the better part of valor. I am not brave but I am not stupid either. Only a fool chooses to fight when he knows he's going to get hurt. My goal is for all my staff go home at the end of the day. If something happens and a staff member has to go to the emergency room, the first thing I ask is, "What did I do wrong?" Then, "What got that person hurt? What could I have done to prevent this injury?" I tell my officers that we will fight when I choose to fight, not when the inmate chooses. Any experienced supervisor usually thinks that way. For some reason the new ones think they have something to prove to the world or to themselves. They just have to do it the hard way. They will laugh and joke about how many staff it took to put someone down. They think it's funny if the inmate has to go out for stitches or a cast. But it isn't so funny a year later when they find out that they are being sued for excessive force.

I was working third shift at the Morgan Street Detention Center, just myself and five officers to three hundred inmates. Four of the officers were on probation, meaning that they were rookies. It was about 1:00 a.m. when I got the call from the block officer that someone was lighting toilet paper and throwing it out on the tier. (Morgan Street has six tiers. All but two were doubles, meaning that each had twelve cells facing each other. Each cell holds two inmates.)

When I got there, the place was a mess. The whole tier was yelling and throwing water, either across the tier at another cell or at the staff. I motioned to the officers to remain at the head of the tier while I took a walk down to survey the damage. I wasn't worried about getting wet or anything like that, for the unit was locked down. What I was looking for were the culprits.

I had several reasons for going alone. First I didn't want the inmates to think that I was the type of supervisor who was going to charge into something blindly with all my staff. Second, sometimes an inmate will do something when he thinks your back is turned. The officer's job was to watch my back. And three, I could move quietly. I could stop and talk or keep going. The mere fact that I walked alone was a way of demonstrating my confidence in my staff and myself.

Bingo! His name was Reilly. I don't recall his first name but we will never forget each other. As I was walking I saw an arm come out of a cell holding a cup of water. The arm then threw the water into the cell across the tier. Now it was my intention just to catch someone, let them know they were caught and have them clean the place up. Then tell them all to go to bed. I wasn't sure who the thrower was until I got to the cell. There were two occupants, one black and the other white. I was looking for a black arm so that narrowed the search down some. I guess he thought I had other plans for him because he became verbally abusive towards me and the staff. He was also foolish enough to refuse to clean the mess up.

I motioned for a couple of officers to join me and told the block officer to open the cell door. The cellmate was in his bunk, covered up and pretending to be asleep. That was his way of saying he was out of it. I told the officers to escort Mr. Reilly out to the bullpen.

Morgan Street had two bullpens. Both were right across from the lieutenant's office. In these were stainless steel benches, a toilet and a sink. The bars went from the floor to the ceiling where they met a steel overhead. These large cells were used for inmates who were going out or returning from court. They were also used as a holding area for medical or maybe the discipline board. The officers placed Reilly in the back bullpen without incident and left him there to chill out.

As soon as they left the area, Reilly started yelling at the top of his lungs. When that got no response he started to sing. Now I won't say that he couldn't sing but I will say that I prefer country music. Getting no response singing, Reilly went to the toilet and sink and turned the water on. In the toilet he shoved his shirt into the pipe and started flushing. As the puddle started spreading, I directed one of the officers to turn the water off at the check valve.

Reilly decided to try to kick the door down. Now we are talking about a door made from one-inch thick steel bars with a massive Folger Adams lock. After about five minutes of this, I decided that a change was in the offing. I took a couple of sets of handcuffs and leg irons and went to pay a call on Mr. Reilly. I told him that if he didn't knock off the racket then I would be forced to chain him down. (Disruptive inmates are sometimes placed in what we call four point restraints. At Morgan Street that meant placing the inmate on the floor and securing him spread eagle to the benches.) I guess he didn't believe me. He made repeated threats about what he was going to do to me if I opened the door. I just shook my head in disgust; we were now past the point of talking.

I told him to back away from the door that we were coming in. He just stood there in an assaultive posture saying, "C'mon mother fucker, I'm going to hurt you."

I repeated my order for him to back away from the door, but he wouldn't move. He kept yelling obscenities. Evaluating the situation, I determined that when we opened the door we were going to have to fight him, so turning away from him I quietly removed my Capstun from its holder and for the last time I told him to back away from the door. When he didn't, I gave him a short burst to the face. He went down like a dropped rock. I motioned the officers out of the area and waited about five minutes for the spray to dissipate.

When we returned, Reilly was sitting on the back bench holding his hands over his eyes. I motioned for an officer to open the door. I prefer to work with my staff by motioning what I want done. I do this because the inmates listen and when they hear what the order is, they can prepare a defense. The problem was, the door wouldn't unlock. I thought he had the wrong key and directed another officer to try. Again nothing. This time I used my key but the lock wouldn't turn. After several attempts with no success I told one of the officers to turn the water back on and yelled to Reilly to splash his eyes with cold water, that it would feel better.

I returned to my office to place a call to the duty maintenance officer. I told him I had an inmate in the bullpen and the lock wouldn't work. I couldn't just leave him there; every inmate must be given a way to exit an area in case of fire. We are responsible for their safety and well being. There must be a way to get to him in an emergency. With that lock jammed he was helpless. The maintenance officer (m/o) said he would be in shortly.

I went back to the bullpen. Reilly had his pants off and was using them to splash his face with water. Unfortunately he was getting water everywhere. Sarcastically, I told him not to make a mess or he would be cleaning it up.

While I was waiting for the m/o, I went back to the block where the officer had an inmate out cleaning. When I walked down the tier, several inmates told me that they were sorry for the mess, that it had just gotten out of hand and that it wouldn't happen again. I just nodded. On my way out, I thanked the worker and asked him to come and see me when he was done. He deserved a cup of coffee.

The m/o got in about two a.m. and had to take the door apart to get Reilly out. I then directed two officers to escort Reilly to the showers. I told them to let him take a shower, get him some clean clothes and a cup of coffee. I also took a minute to show Reilly how to wash his head and face so that the spray didn't run back down in his eyes. As he was walking away I told the officers that I wanted to talk to Reilly before he went to bed.

I went to see him around 3:00 a.m. He was standing by the door of his new cell in segregation. I asked him what that was all about. He said he didn't know; he was just having fun. I asked him about the bull pen fiasco and he told me that he thought we were going to roll up on him and beat him down. I told him I didn't work that way and didn't permit that kind of thing. He nodded, saying "Yeah, now I know." I told him I was concerned about his well being and asked if he wanted to go to medical to be checked out. He said no, he was OK. As I was leaving, he called me back. He said he had learned two things tonight. One, don't fuck with Lt. Dickenson and two, don't fuck with the man in the can. We both laughed and I left.

That I had used the spray on someone was all over the jail within hours. What was more important was the news that after I used it I made sure the inmate was all right, cleaned up and checked out. This is very important with the inmates. It shows professionalism and fairness. There should never be any anger after an incident. It was over and that was that.

Several weeks later when Reilly got out of seg we joked about that night. Eventually he told everyone to give the lieutenant a chance. "See what he wants before you do something stupid."

Several months later, another inmate thought he would try me. Once a week we had hard-boiled eggs for breakfast. This inmate would peel his eggs and throw the shells on the floor. I had spoken to him about it, pointing out that he was not home and the kitchen workers weren't going to pick up after him.

The following week he did it again but this time he was looking right at me when he did it. I just smiled and told him that he had to clean it up before he left the dining area. I thought I detected indecision in his eyes and I had a feeling he needed to save face in front of the other inmates. I told the staff in the mess hall I was going to my office for a minute and to make sure that the foolish inmate remained in the area until I returned. When I was on my way back to the mess hall, I passed Mr. Reilly. With a grin on his face he stopped me and said, "I told him he better do what you say. I warned him, Mr. D. That boy sure is stupid."

I smiled and said, "Thank you, Mr. Reilly, but some people just have to learn the hard way."

I entered the dining hall to find the only person there was the egg man. He was on the floor picking up shells so I didn't say anything and just poured myself a cup of coffee. When he had finished and was leaving, all he said was "Thanks lieutenant." I just nodded. We all need a chance to save our self-respect and maintain our image from time to time.

It doesn't matter how big you are or how tough you think you are when the man in the can is about to speak, everybody listens.

Segregation

I don't claim to be an expert on segregation, but I know it's not a place where inmates want to do their time. According to the department regulations, segregation is to be used as a means of deterring behavioral problems. As the word implies, segregation means to keep away or apart from.

At the old Haddam Jail, the seg unit was not a nice place. The cells were unlit, unheated, and had a hole for sanitary needs. The door was solid except for two small portals, one to view the inmate from time to time and the second, close to the floor, to place food in the cell. Both were kept closed at all times. The inmate only came out when his punishment time was served. There was no bed. The inmate had to sleep on the floor.

At Enfield Medium, the seg cells were in the administration building. There were two sections. One had five cells and the other four — each six by eight. Inside was a metal slab on which a mattress was placed. The inmate got no bedding. One can hang himself with a sheet. The doors were solid here, too, but in this case solid steel. There was a small six-inch square covered with reinforced Plexiglas to look through to check on the inmate. Talking was done through the door. There was a stainless steel toilet and small sink welded to the wall. Running water was kept turned off. When

131

inmates get frisky they like to pack the toilet with paper and flood their cells so that the officer will have a mess and have something to do. If an inmate had to flush the toilet, he had to call to the officer on duty and asks him to turn the water on. If the officer didn't like someone, it could get a little smelly.

The only times the door was opened was during the serving of a meal or for a bi-weekly shower. There are always two officers present when the doors are opened. Also, only one inmate is allowed out at a time. One of the tricks officers pull is to wake an inmate up at 5:00 a.m. and ask if he wants a shower. The usual answer at that time is no. An entry is then made on the seg sheet that the occupant refused, and he won't have a chance again until later that week.

What can you do in seg? Read. You are allowed one book at a time but only three a week. The problem is, you don't get to pick the book; the officer does. When I worked seg I would give an Anglo a book in Spanish to read. I remember one time giving a black inmate a copy of Mein Kampf and a Spanish guy a copy of the Koran. When an inmate asked for a book, I would give him one. Whether he could read it or not was his problem. Some of the other officers would give out a novel with the last three pages torn out. Television, no way. Radio, not on your life. You were not allowed to speak to anyone either.

Gates had the funniest seg unit I ever saw. It was a small five by eight cell in the basement. Unlike most places, this one had bars instead of solid walls or doors. It had a toilet but it was on the outside of the cell so if an inmate wanted to go he had to wait until the officer was around. There was no bed. All you got was a mattress on the floor. That and the clothes you were wearing. What made it funny was the ceiling. It wasn't attached. If you wanted out, all you had to do was to push it up and slide over the top of the bars. I don't remember if anyone ever tried that. If we had to put two people in seg at once, one was on the inside and the other chained to the bars on the outside. Hell of a way to run a jail.

Montville had two seg cells located inside small rooms. The cells were six by six with two metal frames for mattresses. The area between the cell and the outside door was about four feet wide. Once the outside door was closed you could yell your lungs out and no one would hear. Each room had a toilet but again it was on the outside of the bars. The inmates were allowed to come out a couple of times a week for showers but that was it. At one point I remember both rooms full. There were two inmates in each cell and a third chained to the outside of the bars.

Hartford had a great seg unit. It was set off of the medical unit. If I remember correctly, there were eight single cells with nothing in them. Right in the middle was a raised stainless steel platform. If you were a decent occupant of seg, you were allowed to have a mattress and if you weren't, you didn't. There were many occasions when an inmate had to be chained down. This was done when the inmate was totally out of control or assaultive towards staff.

The last person an inmate wants to threaten is the supervisor. Being chained down is not very comfortable. Inmates are placed face down on the steel slab; their arms and legs are spread apart like a cartwheel, with handcuffs and leg irons used to secure them. You can keep an inmate like this for eight to twelve hours, providing a supervisor checks him every four hours. A common practice was for the off-going supervisor to check on the inmate just before shift change. At that time he would do something to the inmate and the inmate would be wound up again. Then the on-coming supervisor along with the off-going one would go down to check the inmate. Upon seeing the off-going supervisor, the inmate would usually become very vocal about what he was going to do when he was let up. The new supervisor would have no choice but to leave him like that for another eight hours. There was no letting them up to go to the bathroom. If they had to go, they held it until they couldn't. Then they lay in it.

The last two cells had full doors. These were the strip cells. Suicide cases found their way here. What made those two cells unbearable was the fact that they were right next to the evacuation door. We were never allowed to open this door but that really wasn't necessary; there was no insulation around it. In the winter, with no clothes, you could get real cold real fast. That was usually enough to break even the roughest occupant.

Here, too, the officer had to turn the water on if inmates needed to flush the toilet. They were allowed out daily to shower but that offer was made either at some ungodly hour of the morning or the middle of the night.

On the other side of the medical unit was the isolation unit, consisting of another eight cells. Each one had a full door with a small window. The rooms were large enough for two fixed beds plus a movable one if needed. The only time we put two people in the same room was if they were both suffering from the same illness. Sometimes these rooms were used for segregation. Either way there was no television, radio, cigarettes or snacks. You were allowed the proverbial book though.

The seg unit at Niantic was a farce. It consisted of two floors — one housing sixteen inmates and the other, twelve. On the first floor, there was one room with a security door. This was supposedly for the problem children. The reason I say seg there was a farce is because no one at Niantic bothered to read the directives concerning the housing of inmates in segregation status.

Niantic was previously called the state farm for women. At the time of its conception, it only housed unwed mothers, adulteresses, sometimes a shoplifter, someone who was arrested for creating a disturbance or other stupid crimes. The old time staff would tell me that there were no criminals there, no bad girls, just misunderstood children.

To that, I'd shout, "Bullshit! We've got three teenagers here, the youngest, sixteen and the oldest, nineteen. In cold blood they murdered a woman who was five months pregnant by stabbing her repeatedly in the abdomen. Make no mistake, these are bad girls!"

There was the leader of a notorious gang called the "Latin Queens" who from her jail cell planned the murders of those who were going to testify against her. There was a mother who sexually molested her three year old son. What about baby bakers, drug dealers, prostitutes or the woman who tried to kill the president of a major surgical company by placing a bomb next to his reserved parking place? Bad girls? Not at Niantic. I should point out that this state did not have a death row for females so they enjoyed walking around privileges at a minimum-security facility which had no perimeter fences.

The seg rooms at Niantic were two person rooms, except one, which was a six-person room. What usually put a girl in seg was stealing or fighting. Fights among the women were a common occurrence due to rampant homosexuality which the administration encouraged under the pretext that a happy girl is not a problem girl. It was common practice to house lovers together. If one of the girls got sent to seg, a day or so later, her lover would do something to be sent there also. The staff usually placed them in the same seg room so there would not be a problem.

When in seg inmates usually get nothing. That wasn't the case at Niantic. The girls were allowed to pack all their clothes, keep their television, radio, cosmetics, and commissary items. All this was allowed in the room. Each girl was allowed to have a tierman job, which meant that they did not spend their time locked up but were allowed to walk around pretending to work.

The staff brought in food, cigarettes, magazines, letters from friends in other housing units, and so forth. There were times that as a supervisor I tried to put a stop to this but after I would leave for the day, another supervisor who was the girls' friend would give her everything. Enforcing the rules according to the department was a waste of time there. In one incident an inmate tried to claim that a hood ornament was a religious medallion. What made it dangerous was that it was on an imitation gold chain made from watchbands. We had to fight to take it from her, and as a result she sued me for violating her civil rights.

A couple of years ago, a new female facility opened. It was supposed to be a maximum-security facility.It doesn't matter how you build a place or what kind of rules you write for it, when you staff it with the same ineffective people from before all you do is bring your problems with you. And that's just what the state did.

Morgan Street had a decent seg unit. There were eight cells, each of them holding two inmates. Unlike most places, the inmates were allowed to wear their prison clothes, have mattresses, sheets and blankets. It was hard for them to have any contraband as the entire unit was shaken down on a daily basis. Staff would remove the occupants and search the cell from top to bottom. All linen and clothes were inspected for tears or shreds. Anything damaged was replaced immediately.

If an inmate was a real problem and had to be restrained it was usually in the holding cell across from the lieutenant's office. The inmate would be spread-eagled on the floor and secured to the benches with leg irons and cuffs, sometimes without clothes.

136

Radgowski correctional had a seg unit but it is now the barbershop. Anytime they have a problem inmate they send him over to Corrigan Correctional. I never worked Corrigan, so I really can't comment on what they do there.

There are other seg units throughout the state and from what I hear some of them are a real bitch to do time in. From the staff's point of view segregation, if run properly, is such a nice place to work.

Movies

Things go full circle. Eleven years ago I started in the old Montville Jail and here I was back again. The only difference was a new building called the Stanley J. Radgowski Correctional Center.

I had been at Morgan Street, but they closed it down and I was transferred back to Niantic. At Niantic, I was called into the deputy warden's office and told in no uncertain terms that I was not wanted there. The deputy told me not to bother even unpacking my coffee cup as I wasn't staying. I didn't get mad or anything like that. I just pointed out that there were eight other lieutenants, all junior to me and that if someone was leaving it had better be one of them.

It is customary for the warden to call all new supervisors into his office and welcome them on board. When I didn't receive a call, I knew for sure that I wasn't wanted there. Despite this minor setback I refused to let them irritate me. For five weeks I tried to fit in as best I could, but it's hard when your heart's not in it.

Anyway, five weeks after my arrival I received a letter via interdepartmental mail from the human resources office telling me that I had just been transferred to Radgowski. I called human resources and told them that I was not the junior lieutenant and that the only way I was going was if I was ordered to in writing. Two days later I received a letter at home ordering me to report. The funny thing about the letter was that the warden didn't even have the balls to sign it himself. He had a secretary do it.

When I got to Radgowski, the captain called me into his office and told me that I would be reporting to third shift. I didn't mind, as all I wanted to do was maintain a low profile for awhile. I waited for a note from the warden giving me the time for my welcome aboard speech but it never came. After almost four weeks I gave up waiting. By not getting a note I deduced that I was not wanted here either, but by now there was nothing new about that.

One of the great (unwritten) policies at the Radgowski Correctional Center was for staff to bring in movies they had rented for the inmates to watch on late nights. This was against every rule I had ever learned working corrections. Under no circumstances is a staff member to bring in or take out anything for the inmates. I guess that didn't apply to movies.

A late night was a Friday or Saturday and sometimes Sunday if Monday was a holiday. On these nights, the inmates were allowed to watch television until two o'clock in the morning or until the movie was finished, whichever was later. It was in fact the cheapest babysitter we had. We figured that as long as they were watching television, they weren't getting into trouble and that's all we ever wanted.

When I took over as shift supervisor I was asked what I would permit in the way of movies. I answered that I would not allow any X-rated movies or any karate or kung fu movies that might wind the inmates up. What I didn't want was someone practicing karate kicks in the middle of the night with the lights off.

Around the end of November, I was approached by one of the officers who asked if he could bring in a movie titled

"Body Chemistry." I asked what it was rated and was told that because it was a pilot film it was listed NR. Figuring that it was a made-for-television movie, I saw no reason not to permit it. Unfortunately, it turned out that the movie has a partial nude scene in it. When this was brought to my attention I really didn't think anything of it; after all, there are partial nude scenes on regular television. What was the big deal?

At that time one female officer was assigned to my shift, and she took exception to the movie. She didn't object at 12:30, when the movie started, but by the end of her shift at 7:30 in the morning Officer Patricia Martin came to me and complained that I had no right subjecting her to that type of conduct by the inmates. I had no idea what she was talking about. She got mad and told me that since I was a male she didn't expect me to understand. I told her that I still had no idea what she was talking about.

She told me she was referring to that movie! I told her that if it had upset her, she should have said something right away and I would have stopped it or had her relieved. To say that the movie upset her is a great understatement. She told me that all night long after the movie, inmates were going to the bathroom and masturbating. I asked how she knew this and if any of the inmates had exposed themselves to her. She replied in the negative but just knew they were doing it. I tried to explain to her that unless someone had exposed himself to her there wasn't a lot I could do. I could see that I wasn't getting anywhere, so it was at this point that I asked her if she wanted to file a complaint. She said, "No, " she was just venting.

Assuming it was over, I put the whole thing out of my mind. Unfortunately, that was a little soon. A couple of days later I was again approached by officer Martin who told me that she hadn't appreciated the comment Officer Spencer had made on the radio about the contents of the movie. I asked her why hadn't she said something about it when we last spoke and she told me that she wasn't sure what she had heard and didn't want to comment on something she wasn't sure about. I told her that it was a little late but that I would look into this and that I was not about to fly off the handle half-cocked until I knew exactly what had been said.

Later that night I called Officer Spencer and he admitted making a comment about the movie's contents. While I was counseling him about radio procedures, Officer Martin barged in and told me that this wasn't over. Like an idiot I asked her what she was talking about, and she hit the roof all over again and stormed out of the office. I went back to business with Officer Spencer and decided to put everything down on paper and give it to the captain.

After I had dismissed Spencer, I fired up the computer and informed the captain and asked for a chance to sit down with him to discuss it. His only response was a short note telling me that there would no longer be any late movies and that he wanted to know who had authorized these late nights. He went on to comment on my abilities as a supervisor for letting the staff bring movies in.

The next night I informed everyone no more movies would be brought in. They wanted to know why and I told them it was because I had said so and that was all there was to it. Some of the other officers wouldn't let it be. Word had gotten around about Martin's being upset and the more they talked among themselves, the more they put two and two together. The bad thing was that they had been overheard by several inmates. Within hours it was all over the jail that Officer Martin was the reason there would be no more movies. Just before breakfast I was again verbally assaulted by Officer Martin. This time she said she didn't appreciate the staff talking about her in front of the inmates. Since I hadn't been part of the conversation I had to plead ignorance and that just set her off all over again.

Three days later, when I returned to work, she told me that several inmates were planning a battery party for her. A battery party is conducted at night when the lights go off. Inmates throw flashlight batteries at the targeted officer in an attempt to knock the officer out. This is very dangerous to all the staff members, not just the target. After roll call I assigned a second officer, Ed Gilbert, to spend a few hours in Martin's unit with her as a back up and as soon as we had completed our midnight count, I sent a third officer down. Unfortunately the only officer I had available was Officer Spencer.

I told Spencer to hang out in Martin's dorm until he was sure there weren't going to be any problems. About thirty minutes later he called me and reported that everything was quiet. I asked if Gilbert was still there and that if he was then Spencer could go ahead with his regular duties. Somewhere around 2:30 a.m., while I was eating, Officer Spencer entered the break room, turned around and asked if I could see the yellow streak on his back? When I didn't respond he asked again. I had to ask what he was talking about. He told me Officer Martin was making comments to other staff that he was a coward and had left her in the dorms by herself. I asked if Officer Gilbert was there when he left and he told me yes. He said if Gilbert hadn't been there he would have stayed.

When Officers Martin and Gilbert entered the break room at about 3:00 a.m., neither of them said anything about the dorm being tense or any batteries being thrown. I asked if everything was OK down there and Martin told me everything was fine. Based on that I decided not to pursue the Spencer remarks.

After I made my rounds, I decided to write the captain again and give him an update. I told him about Martin's comments about Spencer being a coward. I also mentioned

Martin's remarks about the other officers talking about her. I again repeated my request for some guidance concerning the tensions on the shift. This time I received no reply at all.

I decided to send the deputy warden a note on the fourth of December and request a meeting. I told her that I had received no feedback from the captain and that I really needed to speak with someone about this. This time, instead of receiving a reply, I got called to the captain's office. When I entered he threw my note to the deputy at me and told me never to write to her again.

On the thirteenth of December, Officer Collins handed me an incident report in which he said Martin had made some very lewd remarks about his new dog. In commenting on how much the dog cost, Martin said for that much money the dog had better perform oral sex on Collins on a regular basis. The report went on to say that another supervisor had been present during the conversation. Officer Collins told me that he felt very uncomfortable hearing a woman make comments of that nature and he had no choice but to report it. I asked Collins what exactly was going on here. After much hesitation he told me his report was in response to Martin's complaint regarding the movie and staff talking about her. He told me in confidence that most of the shift was really pissed at her for screwing up a good thing and went on to say that she couldn't have it both ways. If she was going to be offended by a movie, then she had better clean up her language.

Little did I know that Martin had been to see the deputy warden. I have no idea what they spoke about, but I do know that the deputy called me into her office and chewed me out for not rectifying the morale problem on my shift. The deputy decided to take it upon herself to contact the affirmative action people in Hartford. In her eyes, we had a major sexual harassment case here and she figured to make a name for herself by uncovering it and appearing as the great savior. I might add that she did this without notifying the warden or going through the chain of command — the same chain of command I got counseled about in another incident less than two weeks later.

The third week in December, the affirmative action people launched an investigation into alleged sexual harassment complaints lodged not by Martin but by the deputy warden. In my reports to the captain I had mentioned that this same type of incident had occurred at Martin's last facility. The deputy interpreted this remark to mean that I had something against women in corrections and was taking it out on Martin. She passed that on to the affirmative action people, too.

Starting in January, everyone on the third shift was to be interviewed. The officer who had brought the movie in wasn't scheduled until May. He was so rattled by this that he retained a lawyer just for the interview. The lawyer had viewed the movie in question and pointed out to the investigators that Martin's complaint about the movie was groundless. He then went on the offensive and asked what their opinion of the movie was. It turned out that neither of the investigators had bothered to watch it. The lawyer said he was going to advise his client to pursue action against the deputy and Officer Martin for undue stress and harassment. Their goal was to recover expenses. The lawyer's bill was just over three thousand dollars and he figured that the major cause of all this stress was the deputy warden.

My turn came the second week in May. As the subject of an investigation, I should have been advised of my rights. Apparently, no one bothered to tell them that employees have rights, and I wasn't going to point out their oversight. I was already planning an appeal if necessary. The interview went okay until they started rewriting my statement to meet their needs. After much debate, I finally lost my patience and asked them what they thought they were accomplishing. I told them that on three separate occasions I had written my superiors asking for help in dealing with the situation and that if my supervisors would have responded in a timely manner, this would never have escalated to this point.

It seems that my request to the deputy was the one that broke the camel's back. I told the people from Hartford that she never responded but gave the request to the captain. When the captain yelled at me never to write something like that to the deputy again, I had told him that when he hadn't answered my requests I had no choice but to go higher.

By now I was really pissed and somehow got sidetracked. I proceeded to tell them about an instructor at the training academy using foul language, making racial slurs, and remarks of a sexual nature during his classes. I told them that they should be looking into that instead of wasting their time on this. They told me that no one had ever complained about that instructor. Bullshit! I told them I had filed a complaint in writing to the commissioner's office back in January and nothing was being done about it. The instructor was still teaching and I was labeled a troublemaker.

I never did give them a statement. As it turned out, they took the letters that I sent the captain and substituted them for a statement. I asked them again as they were leaving if they were going to look into my complaint and neither of them had an answer. As they left, the older gentleman came back to me and whispered that maybe I was the wrong color to be making such a complaint! I was flabbergasted. I tried to recall if the affirmative action guidelines specified that you had to be a specific race or sex in order to lodge a complaint. I didn't think so, but I wasn't sure so I didn't say anything more. Later that day I checked and found that according to the directives the action or language merely had to be offensive to someone in order to warrant a complaint.

By June, I hadn't heard any more about the movie incident or the instructor. Staff no longer brought in movies; the recreation director now picked the movies and there were a lot of "R" rated movies containing nudity, profanity and violence coming in. I just sat back waiting for the next complaint. We still do late nights around here.

Last week, Officer Martin was abruptly transferred to another shift. There was some friction between her and the other officers. It had something to do with how she thought things should be done and this caused her unnecessary stress, or something along those lines.

Did any of this accomplish anything? Of course it did. We successfully wasted five months of commuting between Hartford and Montville, not to mention countless hours of overtime while staff sat around waiting to be interviewed, or a half dozen trees for the paper required to accommodate the statements and related inter-departmental memos and faxes.

While all this was going on, the incident at the training center had taken place and I filed the complaint about the instructor whom I perceived to be in violation of the affirmative action guidelines.

All I learned out of this is that only selected people can be offended. If you are a white male in this system you can only be the offender, not the offended.

There are some days when this job really sucks!

We got a memo informing us that there would no longer be any movies on late nights starting the first of July. The only thing I could make of this is that the administration would rather have the inmates gambling or who knows what than sitting quietly watching television.

Then, on July third, I received a letter from the deputy warden informing me that I was scheduled for a pre-disciplinary hearing on the twelfth. The letter went on to say that I was facing a suspension for the sexual harassment of Officer Martin. I can't believe it! I'm going to be suspended for reporting an incident!

A pre-disciplinary hearing is called a Lauderhill. When my Lauderhill hearing took place, someone forgot about the employee rights form. The deputy conducted the hearing along with someone from personnel and a captain. I asked the deputy why we were doing this as the affirmative action people had found me not guilty. She told me that since their investigation was concluded she could now conduct her own administrative investigation. I asked when this investigation was starting and she told me that it had already been completed. I was flabbergasted. Completed! When were the interviews done and when was it my turn? She told me that she had used my letters as my statement, that the investigation was closed and she wasn't going to discuss it. During the Lauderhill we ended up arguing over who was really at fault and who had been negligent in their duties. The deputy didn't like the results of Hartford's investigation, so she did her own and found me guilty. As it turned out I was to be disciplined for violating the administrative directives regarding things coming in or going out for inmates and sexual harassment of Patricia Martin by knowing that she had a nickname.

Two weeks later, I received a letter of reprimand for showing poor judgment. The funny thing about the letter was that it was issued on August 26, 1996 and said the offense occurred on November 27, 1996! Can you believe it; I was disciplined for an offense that had not yet occurred.

The Old Boys' Network

A while back I had a great opportunity to see first hand the old boys' network in action. I knew it existed, but it was really enlightening to see how well it worked I don't believe I shall ever trust in the system again.

The Department of Corrections has some really great rules. Unfortunately, they are selectively enforced. Who you are, where and with whom you have worked, determines what rules apply to you.

Over the years I've seem inmates mercilessly beaten and never a report filed. On the other hand, I saw a staff member improperly use a restraint hold and end up being disciplined for excessive force. In the case where the staff member beat the inmate, all that was said was "Well, that's Johnny Jones. That's the way he learned and he has always been that way. He's never going to change." To me that's not an acceptable explanation. If you're doing something wrong, someone should bring it to your attention and advise you to change. If you don't change, then the necessary action should be taken. At least that's what the rules say, but then again, the rules don't apply to some people.

I was disciplined two years ago for using obscene language in the presence of female inmates. I had been assigned to a new female detention center as a supervisor. We were a new facility, which meant we were doing and learning from scratch and as with every new operation, there are foul-ups. Meals arrive late, visiting lists are not accurate, commissary either arrives early or not at all, the laundry breaks down or linen exchange gets screwed up. Anyway I don't recall exactly what the foul up was but my immediate response was to say, "What the fuck?!"

My mistake was to say it in the presence of some inmates and the warden. The inmates didn't mind; they use the word all the time. The warden on the other hand took exception. I could go on about the warden here, but I've already done that. Suffice it to say that the warden was relieved due to incompetence and demoted, then demoted again. Now he is junior to me.

Anyway, I was called in to the warden's office several days later and given formal counseling regarding inappropriate language around inmates. Formal counseling means that an entry is made into my record implying a discipline problem. When I asked about the times that the inmates used that word around me, I was told that it was okay because they talk that way. That's right, I can't say it but they can. That explanation did not sit well with me and I voiced my opinion accordingly. All that did was get me in more trouble.

Getting back to the story of the old boys' network, I was assigned to the training academy for supervisors' training in the use of firearms. I knew most of the people there, some by name and others by face, and they knew me. After all, I was labeled a troublemaker. Keith Johnson was the instructor and we didn't get along well. That is stating the case with a great deal of reservation.

The class started late as usual. Nothing in this department ever starts on time. For the first hour, Keith stood in the front of the room and commented on everything and anything, preceding most of his statements with the word "fuck." It was

149

"this fucking thing" or it was "fucked up" or just plain "fuck."
I was a little surprised to hear an instructor use that type of
language in front of a class, especially a mixed gender class.
I thought it was uncalled for. I didn't say anything, for I kept
expecting one of the captains in the class to say something to
Keith about his language, but no one did.

As the day progressed, Keith made repeated remarks
about a black rapper called Sneaky Weasel. Sneaky was on
trial for a drive-by shooting in California. What made it
exceptional was that Sneaky and his bodyguard drove
around the block several times waiting for the victim to
come out of the bar. In the course of their travels, Sneaky
repeatedly waved to his fans, which is not the most intelligent thing to do when you're planning a drive by. Whenever
someone in the class did something wrong, or what Keith
considered stupid, he would ask them if they were related to
Sneaky Weasel. I took this to be a racial slur and waited for
someone to say something. I figured that one of the blacks in
the class would finally say enough is enough. I was wrong
again.

We broke for lunch and I asked the lieutenant I was with if
he had felt the remarks were inappropriate, or if he took
exception to them? "Inappropriate, yes," he said, "exception,
no." He said he thought I was over-reacting, so I dropped the
subject.

The afternoon session continued in the same vein.
Obscenities and off color remarks. Now I knew one lady in
the room from having worked with her at Niantic several
years before and figured she would say something but she
never did. the final straw was when Keith said something to
the class and Sharon nodded her head in agreement. Keith
looked right at her and said, "Sharon, just nod your head
once. Any more than that and I get excited."

I was stunned! I couldn't believe what I had just heard. A

remark like that in mixed company from an instructor! I expected Sharon to tear him up but she said nothing.

As I was driving home I kept thinking about the class and the instructor's language. I remembered my counseling and having to listen while the warden reminded me that the department had specific rules about comments of that nature. The more I thought about it, the madder I got until I just couldn't let it go anymore. Now I knew Keith had friends and I knew my warden and captain were among them. And I felt that by going through them I would accomplish nothing, so I chose to go directly to the boss.

I knew that I had to inform my superiors in the process, so what I did was type up my complaint and fax it from my home to the director of training at the academy, then to the director of the region, then to my warden and finally to the commissioner himself. But I did not list each one in the "copies to" section. By them not knowing that someone else had also been notified it was going to be interesting to see who would try to cover this up. I did all this at about 5:00 p.m. so when they got to their offices the next morning it was right there.

I got the expected results. Because none of them knew about the others, each of the recipients thought they would make some discreet phone calls, keep this quiet to protect a friend and I would go away. Surprise, surprise, it ain't that easy. One of the calls I received was from the senior captain at the academy, assuring me that they would look into this and get back to me shortly. That was three months ago. I received a letter from the director of the region informing me that he had received my complaint and I could be assured that the appropriate action would be taken. That too was three months ago. I was then contacted by internal affairs and was told that the Commissioner had instituted an investigation and that as the complainant I would be informed within thirty days as to the outcome. That was two and a half months ago. I was then contacted by my captain and told that this was a dumb move on my part. What had I been thinking about? Didn't I know Keith had friends in high places? I said yes but that Keith had been wrong. I received a discreet warning from the captain to drop it.

Several weeks later I was disciplined by my warden for going outside the chain of command. Again I received a formal counseling along with a direct order that under no circumstances was I to speak with anyone outside the facility without going through the captain first. I guess Keith really does have friends in high places and they do bend over backwards to look out for one another.

From this incident I have learned that just being right does not make you right. And being wrong is all right as long as you know the right people. And that rules are like clouds, they appear big and impressive but have little substance if you know the right people. I have found also that the Department of Corrections adheres to a rigid policy of selective enforcement regarding its rules.

I had coffee with a close friend a couple of weeks ago and told him about the incident. He suggested that I should contact my warden and explain that I was only trying to comply with the department's guidelines. That I regretted going over his head but I thought because Keith worked at the academy that I should submit my complaint to his boss. He suggested that I point out I had been disciplined for such conduct in the past and believed that I was doing the right thing. The warden has refused to meet with me.

Hindsight

There is no bitterness in me right now, only acquiescence. I said when I began this book that it was a way of venting, but the more I wrote, the more bitter I became. Every time I recalled a person who for some reason ended up in these pages, my mood would change. Most of the time I just got mad, but sometimes — not very often, but sometimes — I would smile.

I so much wanted to be part of the team. I wanted to be able to stop after work and maybe tip a few with my fellow officers. I wanted to laugh with them, to tell jokes or just be a part of them. Instead, on the way home I tried to figure where I went wrong.

I am not going to blame only the system for the way everything turned out. I contributed to my own agony. I had set high standards for everyone, including myself. I chose not to share my feelings with my wife. I thought that I was strong enough to be able to carry it all myself. I was wrong.

I don't have any advice for new staff on how to avoid any of this, other than to find another profession. They say that hindsight is 20/20 and in a way I guess it is. I do know that if I had it to do all over again, I wouldn't.

Does anybody know if the local hamburger place is hiring?

Glossary

AC/DC: An inmate who is bi-sexual.

Admin. Directives: Directives issued by the department which are meant to serve as the laws governing the conduct of both inmates and staff.

Amy: A name given to a very feminine homosexual. Usually very young with fair complexion and long hair, this prisoner would easily be mistaken for a woman on the streets.

A/P: Admissions and processing. Every prisoner assigned to the facility must enter through the a/p area. New admits are stripped, showered, de-loused, and photographed before being assigned a housing unit. Inmates on outside work details must also pass through the a/p area but are only strip searched before being allowed to return to their units.

Baby baker: This is an expression used to describe a female inmate doing time for killing her child when the newborn was placed in a gas oven with the pilot light off and the gas on. Most times the crime is committed within several weeks of birth when the woman is suffering from post-partum depression.

Battery party: Inmates will throw batteries at a staff's head often after the lights have gone out or the officer's back is turned. To warrant this kind of attention, the officer has probably done something to cause the population to lose a privilege.

Beat down: To beat someone down means that a group of either staff or population will converge to punch and kick the victim to a submissive position on the floor.

Bible: The unit log.

Bid: The length of a sentence.

Black box: This is a hard plastic box that fits over the chain of a pair of handcuffs restricting movement of the chain and the hands. In the center of the box is a slot through which a long chain is passed. The chain is then wrapped around the inmate's waist and secured with a padlock to prohibit the inmate from raising his hands. This type of device is used when transporting assaultive or disruptive inmates.

Body alarm: A small transmitter worn by the staff on duty. Each has a signature signal which is assigned to a particular officer. The better ones look like a fat ball point pen. In the vertical position it is in the stand-by mode. If the officer is knocked down or the alarm is thrown down, the mercury switch is activated and an alarm sounds in the control center. Once this occurs "an officer needs assistance" is called over the radio along with a location. The less dependable ones look like a pager and have to be manually activated.

Body armor: Used by inmates if they know they are going to be part of a gang fight. Items used for this purpose are several layer of newspapers or magazines taped to the front and back of the torso. Such layers of paper serve as good protection against razor shanks and stiletto type shanks.

Brass: A supervisor: lieutenant, captain, deputy warden or warden.

Bubble: The officers' cubicle. This is supposed to be a secure area where the officer can seek refuge if there is a major disturbance in the unit. It gets its name from the self locking door and reinforced glass windows. Even while in the bubble the officer can observe the entire unit.

Bullpen: A large very secure area, usually found in the admissions area of a facility. Consists of one-inch thick steel bars extending from floor to ceiling with metal ceilings. There is a small metal sink and toilet to accommodate the prisoners. If a facility does not have a designated segregation area, the bullpen is used for this purpose.

Cap Housing: capacity set by court order as the result of lawsuits brought by inmates to prohibit over crowding.

Capstun: This is an oleoresin-based spray used to subdue violent prisoners. The effect is instantaneous on the eyes and mucus membranes. Causing no permanent damage, the effect will wear off naturally in about forty-five minutes.

Caught out: Used by staff and inmates alike, this expression means that you lose.

Cell extraction: Used by staff when referring to the forcible removal of an inmate from a cell block. This type of force is only used when the inmate has gone off or is a threat to himself. Using a convex or concave shield five staff are assigned to rush the inmate once the cell door is opened. The first officer uses the shield to force the inmate against the wall. Each of the other four have specified targets to gain control of. One and two officers grab the left and right arms. Three and four officers go for the legs. Once the extremities are subdued the inmate is placed face down on the floor and restraints applied. Now it is possible to move the inmate with minimal risk to staff.

C.E.R.T: This stands for Correctional Emergency Response Team. Connecticut has a rather extensive, well-trained C.E.R.T. organization. Each facility has staff assigned to this team. Mobilization can be implemented in less than ninety minutes and deployment anywhere in the state in less than an hour. C.E.R.T. is the primary response unit for any facility-wide incident.

Chit: A small metal tag with an officer's name on it. When the officer draws a set of keys or restraints, a chit is placed on the corresponding hook in the control center to reflect who has possession. Upon being relieved from a post the relieving officer gives to off-going officer a chit which is then substituted for the original.

Classification: An inmate's custody level. An inmate or prisoner can have their classification level raised or lowered depending on their length of sentence and conduct.

Code: A term used by staff. Rather than have visitors get upset when an officer calls for an institutional emergency, the department went to a color code system. Blue means officer needs assistance. Red denotes fire. Green refers to an escape. White indicates medical. Orange means riot.

Commissary: Items purchased by prisoners from the facility store. Such items include but are not limited to candy, cigarettes, soap, tea, coffee, powdered beverages, envelopes, pens and writing paper.

157

Contraband: Any item found in an inmate's possession or in an area occupied by inmates that has not been issued by the state or not obtainable through the commissary.

Control: From this area, all of the minute to minute functions of the facility are coordinated. Manned twenty-four hours a day, this post is normally located in the most secure part of the facility. Jammed with countless video monitors, all electric doors and gates are operated from this area.

Convict: A prisoner who has done some major time: twenty years or more. Convicts believe themselves to be superior to inmates. A convict will never look you in the eye. Anytime they speak to you it will be in a public area with other convicts around. The volume of talk will always be loud enough to be overheard so that there can be no mistaking about what is being said. They will always keep a minimum of five feet between you so that they can never be accused of snitching anyone out. A convict is very neat and always maintains a very correct appearance. A convict will appear almost anti-social, associating only with other convicts. When not at an assigned work detail a convict will always remain in close proximity to his bunk or cell. Convicts will always address staff as mister or miss.

Count: A head count of prisoners. Prisoners are required to return to their respective housing units at various times so that the facility can insure there have been no escapes. Each shift is required to conduct at least one formal count and two informal counts. The formal count is logged in the facility log and passed on to the administrative offices to facilitate the movement of prisoners between facilities.

C/O: Corrections officer

Cowboy: Also referred to as a John Wayne; this is an officer who goes around looking for trouble. When staff is accused of excessive force it's usually because of cowboys. After a fight, they'll brag about how they hurt an inmate. Cowboys never see themselves this way. They justify their actions by saying that they are "just doing their job.'

Crate: An expression used when referring to a carton of cigarettes.

D.H.O: Discipline Hearing Officer.

Diesel: An inmate "pumping up" or body building.

Dime dropper: This is a snitch, stool pigeon, informant. The word dime refers to the ten days in seg someone receives after being snitched out for a violation.

Drafted: Also meaning frozen. This term is used by staff to indicate that someone will not be able to leave at the end of their shift because not enough relieving staff reported for duty.

D/R: Discipline Report. This is a report that details prisoner misconduct so that the D.H.O. can award a fair discipline in an attempt to correct unwanted behavior.

E.O.S: End Of Sentence. Time Served.

Eye in the sky: Surveillance cameras mounted on the ceilings.

Family album: A rolodex file. In this file are cards on every inmate in the unit. Information contained on the cards includes name, number, picture, bed number and job. Up until about five years ago there could also be a red dot in the upper left corner. This dot was to warn staff that this person had Aids or was HIV positive.

Flex cuffs: Reinforced nylon straps used in lieu of handcuffs. Able to withstand severe stress, they can only be used once and can only be removed by cutting the strap itself.

Fly bad: An inmate expression. When someone is said to "fly bad, " it means that they are either good in the population's eyes or doing something that the population thinks warrants merit.

Four points: Restraining a prisoner spread eagle on a bunk and applying handcuffs and leg irons. This is only done when the prisoner is creating such a disruption as to destroy the contents of their cell or inflict injury on themselves.

Frisk search: A quick pat down of an inmate who has been randomly selected in an effort to control the movement of contraband.

Gas up: Get lost. Inmates will tell each other to gas up when they think that the other person is drawing unwanted attention.

Goon squad: This name officially surfaced in this state when used by a former commissioner. He used the term in a news conference when referring to staff that had responded to a call for help. There had been claims of excessive force by this squad of goons. The commissioner assured the press that this state did not have goon squads in its facilities nor did it condone the use of excessive force no matter what the circumstances.

Go off: An inmate is said to go off when they become disruptive. In most cases these situations become physical confrontations between staff and inmates.

Greens: Inmate clothing. Sentenced inmates wear green or blue uniforms. Unsentenced inmates wear brown or tan uniforms.

Hot pot: This is usually a large thirty cup coffee pot with the insides removed. This hot water enables the inmates to make instant coffee, tea, or soup. Such pot is kept away from the officer's station to prevent it being dumped on the officer without warning.

House mouse: This is a prisoner who constantly remains in his or her cell. This person needs to watched closely as they will avoid any contact with other prisoners. This condition is an indicator of major depression that usually leads to an attempt to end one's life.

Incident report: I/R. This report is for reporting anything out of the ordinary. Information contained on this form includes but is not limited to, inmate's name and number, housing unit, reporting staff, responding staff and witnesses, detailed description of what happened and final outcome, and the disposition of any contraband or evidence collected.

Informal: An informal is a form of discipline. It is used by staff to correct minor infractions. Its sanctions include loss of commissary, mail, recreation, confinement to quarters, extra duty and other sanctions to be specified by the supervisor.

Inmate: In the old days this would normally be a prisoner who is serving ten years or less. It also could refer to someone who has yet to be sentenced. Inmates are snitches and punks who will do anything if they think they can get something from staff in return.

Jewelry: Another word for restraints. Handcuffs, leg irons, etc.

Juice: "Juice card, " "J.U. ice." Long before facilities allowed commissary, Cool aide or fruit juice was used as a reward for inmates. Those who had regular jobs were given a juice pass. This pass allowed them to come out of their housing unit after supper and receive a cup of juice. If a special job came up during the day and it was done particularly well, the supervising officer would give the inmate a laminated card (juice card) which also permitted the bearer to come out. Eventually it came to mean an inmate receiving something extra from an officer. To have a juice card or some juice is looked on as a status symbol.

Kicken: Used to refer to a new inmate who is still detoxing from the street.

Kite: A note passed between prisoners. It gets its name from the fact that it is usually folded very tightly and thrown to the recipient as he passes a cell.

Lockdown: All prisoners locked in their housing units for a length of time to facilitate the restoration of order. Lockdowns are also used when a facility shakedown has been called for. If a facility is locked down, the population is fed in house rather than in the dining hall.

Lock-n-sock: A padlock in a sock. It is swung like a blackjack. Such a blow can result in a fatality.

Looking out: Used by prisoners to refer to keeping a watch on an officer so that something illegal can be done.

Med line: Four times a day medications are dispensed. A medical staff and a medication cart are escorted by three or four officers to each housing unit. Prisoners needing meds at that time are allowed to line up at the door and receive their medication. The only unit where this is not done is in the seg unit where the medical staff delivers medicine to individual cells.

M.O.A.B: Management of Aggressive Behavior. Class taught to all staff to lessen chance of physical confrontation with prisoners.

New admit: A new admission to the facility.

New jack: An inmate who is doing his/her first time in jail. This term is also used to refer to new staff.

No call/no show: When a staff fails to show up for duty and has not called to report absence. A no call or no show usually result in a staff member being frozen or held over for a second shift.

Oil down: Prior to a fight with staff or a cell extraction, inmates cover their bodies with baby oil or grease from the kitchen making it very difficult for staff to gain control. Baby oil is also poured on the floor just inside the door of a cell. As the staff rush in, they lose their footing enabling the inmate to inflict injury on them while they are helpless.

One on one: Denotes a prisoner's custody status. When a prisoner is extremely suicidal or has demonstrated total disregard for his or her personal well being, he or she is placed on a one on one status. This means that an officer is assigned around the clock. Due the verbal abuse from the prisoner, this post can be emotionally devastating so an officer is not normally permitted to perform this duty any longer than eight hours and not more than two days in a row.

One ringer: Quite common at larger facilities, this is done by staff on duty to let each other know that the supervisor is making his rounds. After the supervisor leaves a unit that officer will call the next unit in line on the phone and let it ring just once. This gives the next unit a heads up.

On the brick: An inmate term meaning discharged or out on the street.

Pack in: This is a term used when directing staff to move a disruptive prisoner. Originating at facilities which have work release or furloughs, it refers to packing all the prisoner's belongings in a plastic bag and moving the prisoner back inside the facility proper. It can also mean placing the belongings in storage while the prisoner is in segregation or restrictive housing.

Pain compliance: A term used by staff when referring to the techniques used on an inmate who has refused to follow simple instructions during a physical confrontation. Pain is applied to various pressure points until the required result is achieved

Patdown: A very quick running of the hands over an inmate who is usually on his way back from a detail or school.

Personal space: An invisible circle around a person which extends about three feet out from the body. Most people get very uncomfortable when a stranger violates this space. a prisoner's locker and bunk are included in his personal space.

Picture frame: Inmates will make picture frames or mirror frames from gum or cigarette wrappers. These are then sold or bartered. They are also seen as a symbol of an inmate's juice because gum is illegal and to get wrappers means that you have a pet officer who brings them in.

Population: The number of prisoners in a facility.

Protective custody: As the word implies, this is done for protective reasons. A prisoner may find himself/herself in P/C for any of the following: testimony against another prisoner, witness protection or suicide attempts.

Pruno: Homemade alcohol. Prisoners hoard sugar and smuggle bread and juice out of the kitchen. They mix in the fruit served with the morning meal, place everything in a plastic bag or container and allow it to ferment for several weeks. Once the container is opened, detection is fairly easy due to its smell. Because raisins would accelerate the fermenting process, they are not permitted in the institutions.

Pull urine: To run a drug test on someone by having them urinate in a sterile container. The expression "piss em" is also used.

Rabbit: A prisoner with an escape history.

Restraints: Any device used to restrict the movement of an inmate's arms and legs, these can be any number of items ranging from basic handcuffs to the more elaborate belly chains. Also in this category are leg irons and black boxes. Reinforced nylon straps called flex cuffs are usually used when an extremely large number of inmates are involved or if the inmate has wrists and ankles too large for normal restraints.

Ripper: A rapist.

Roll up on: When a prisoner has violated the facility's unwritten laws or done something which results in a serious situation, the other prisoners will inflict their own discipline in the form of a beat down.

Room with a view: Segregation. It's meant sarcastically as segregation cells have no windows. The only view you have is four brick walls.

Sallyport: An entrance or exit to a facility consisting of two doors. One of these doors must remain locked at all times. Both doors are reinforced and electrically controlled from an isolated area.

Salt/Seed: Letting some form of contraband be found so that a more serious item will not be discovered by staff.

Segregation: Violent or disruptive prisoners are placed in seg-regation or *seg* for a length of time in an attempt to cor-rect unwanted behavior. In some cases seg is used as a place to house inmates who are in protective custody. Any inmate in seg is automatically placed on what is called a seg sheet. On this sheet are placed thirty-minute entries regarding the inmate's conduct. The shift supervisor must make at least one entry on each sheet once a shift.

Shakedown: A search of a prisoner's property or area. As a precaution, staff are usually assigned to a shakedown in pairs. This permits one officer to search while the other keeps watch. A facility shakedown involves two shifts and any support staff on duty.

Shank: A homemade knife sharpened by scraping on the con-crete floor. Sometimes made from a steel rod but most times from a piece of flat steel or iron. Masking tape is wrapped around the un-sharpened end to act as a handle. Shanks can range anywhere from three to fifteen inches long. Two of the more common methods of making shanks are:

1. Using the blade removed from a disposable razor, a toothbrush handle is warmed until the plastic becomes pli-able. The blade is then inserted in the warm plastic. Once the plastic cools, this becomes a very formidable weapon.

2. A ballpoint pen is disassembled. The metal filler is attached to the outside of the barrel of the pen using masking tape. The metal filler now protrudes about three inches. Again if used against the throat or eyes the results can be tragic.

Sharps: Scissors, kitchen knives, various maintenance tools. Sharps are always kept on a shadow board in a cabinet locked at all times.

Skid: A new inmate in the system. A new inmate doesn't realize that a roll of toilet paper is like gold. On admission, an experienced inmate will right away hoard a roll. The new inmate will usually do without for several days. Skid refers to the marks in a pair of underwear.

Snitch: An inmate who reports on other inmates. In the old days, snitches used to receive good time or time off their bid in exchange for substantiated information, whether it be on staff or other inmates. Now the information is exchanged for little perks.

Soap art: In facilities where full bars of soap are given out you will find some very beautiful soap carvings. Bars of soap are placed together to form a large block. Then using a nail file from a pair of nail clippers, inmates create a sculpture ranging from a simple name to a Santa Claus and reindeer. These sculptures are given as presents to family members. Soap shavings are collected and used in the washing machines when no powdered soap is available.

S.R.G.: Security Risk Group. Members of a S.R.G. are gang members. Gangs include Latin King, Los Solidos, 20 Love, Blood, Crypt, among others.

Stinger: A device used by inmates consisting of two wires plugged into an outlet with a small connecting wire between them. The connecting wire heats ups quickly and permits the inmate to light a cigarette. A similar device is used to heat coffee or tea.

Strip search: A detailed search of a naked prisoner. During this process not only are the clothes searched but the prisoner is required to reveal all cracks and crevices of the body. Female prisoners are required to squat down and cough. Doing this allows anything hidden in a body cavity to be ejected.

Store: A store is a form of black marketing. Run by an inmate, goods usually consist of candy, cigarettes, soap, cosmetics and food. The going rate is two for one. If you borrow a candy bar then you must pay back two on the next commissary day. If you can't pay your debt right then, you now have two and must pay back four. Looked upon as contraband and unauthorized, enforcement of the payback policy is strictly enforced by the store operator.

Stroll: An officer's rounds. To tour the unit is to take a stroll.

Suicide watch: Also known as a Q-15. This means that the prisoner must be checked on at least every fifteen minutes. An entry then has to be made on the seg sheet.

Super max: A high-risk facility. In this type of facility every moment of the prisoners' day is observed and controlled. No prisoner movement is allowed without a supervisor's approval, maximum restraints and a four-man escort.

Tent: A tent is a towel, blanket, or sheet that is hung from the bunk above or from the bars of a cell. A tent is used to block out the lights or afford a certain amount of privacy for unauthorized activities. Tents are prohibited because they obstruct the officer's view.

Tierman: This is an expression that has carried over from the older larger facilities. Those facilities consisted mostly of cellblocks called tiers. A low risk inmate would be selected as a cleaner for that particular tier, considered a privileged position. This inmate usually was assigned to the first cell on that tier. This served two functions. One it was easy for the officer to find him when something needed to be done and second it enabled the inmate to overhear conversations and pass messages or overheard tips to other inmates.

Thorazine shuffle: Until about ten years ago, Thorazine was the drug of choice in correctional facilities. Administered by the medical department, Thorazine is used to control violent prisoners. A prisoner on Thorizine maintains a constant dazed state. The shuffle comes from the sound their feet make when they walk. People under the influence of Thorazine lack any will of their own. This policy of keeping prisoners in a drugged state has been discontinued in most facilities.

Tree jumper: A child molester. The name comes from the old concept that most child molesters would hide in the bushes or trees then leap out and grab a child on the way to or from school.

Trip the block: An officer's rounds.

Use of Force: This is a form that must be completed every time a staff member is forced to lay hands on an inmate. The information required is what happened to require the force, what type of force was used and by whom.

Unit directives: Directives issued by the warden at each facility which serve as guidelines for daily operations.

Victim notification: The notification of a crime victim whenever the perpetrator is being considered for a change in custody status.

Works: Drug paraphernalia.